25 more bags to knit

25 more bags to knit

BEAUTIFUL BAGS IN STYLISH COLOURS

Emma King

COLLINS & BROWN

This book is dedicated to Mum and Pete

First published in the United Kingdom in 2007 by
Collins & Brown Limited
151 Freston Road
London
W10 6TH

An imprint of Anova Books Company Ltd

COMMISSIONING EDITOR: **Michelle Lo**
DESIGN MANAGER: **Gemma Wilson**
EDITOR: **Katie Hudson**
DESIGNER: **Ben Cracknell Studio**
PHOTOGRAPHER: **Mark Winwood**
CHART ILLUSTRATIONS: **Kuo Kang Chen**
PATTERN CHECKER: **Tracy Chapman**
STYLIST: **Ella Bradley**
SENIOR PRODUCTION CONTROLLER: **Morna McPherson**

ISBN-13: 978-1-843403-72-2
ISBN-10: 1-843403-72-2

A CIP catalogue for this book is available from the British Library.

10 9 8 7 6 5 4 3 2 1

Reproduction by Anorax
Printed and bound by Imago, Thailand

This book can be ordered direct from the publisher. Contact the
marketing department, but try your bookshop first.

www.anovabooks.com

Contents

Introduction

It's a well known fact that you can never have too many bags – and if you are a knitter, too many knitted bags! In my latest book, *25 More Bags to Knit,* I wanted to carry on from where I left off with my first book of knitted bags by designing a whole new collection of projects.

I have divided the book into three sections – Anytime, Weekend and Evening. With bags ranging from large weekend totes to chic evening purses, my objective was to create something for every occasion! There are simple knits as well as more complicated ones incorporating techniques such as knitting with colour, beads, sequins and embroidery.

To ensure that a professional finish is achieved I have included full lining instructions with every project, making each design not just stylish but practical too.

As I've said before, my inspiration is always colour and texture and with so many wonderful yarns available, it has been a joy to produce this collection. I hope you enjoy knitting my designs and don't forget, there's nothing to stop you knitting all 25!

emma king

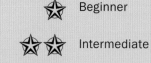 Beginner

Intermediate

 Advanced

These are a guide only. What some knitters find difficult, others find quite easy, so read the pattern before deciding whether or not to knit it.

Anytime

Fleur

Mix it up with this playful day bag and make every trip an enjoyable one. A fusion of tweed and plain yarn add a little seriousness, while an eye-catching floral corsage makes it blooming marvellous. The result? A unique bag brimming with youthful individuality.

SIZE
46cm at widest point × 35cm (18in × 14in)

MATERIALS
4.5mm (US 7) needles
3.25mm (US 3) needles

Yarn
Rowan Summer Tweed
50g (1¾oz) balls
528 Brilliant (A)　　　　　　2

Rowan All Seasons Cotton
50g (1¾oz) balls
203 Giddy (B)　　　　　　　2

Rowan Handknit Cotton
50g (1¾oz) balls
303 Sugar (C)　　　　　　　1

Rowan Kid Silk Haze
25g (1oz) balls
579 Splendour (D)　　　　　1

Wooden Bag handles
(Rowan Z075000-00403)
2 pieces, each measuring
61cm × 50cm (24in × 20in) lining
and wadding fabric (approximately)

TENSION (GAUGE)
17 sts and 25 rows to 10cm (4in)
using 4.5mm (US 7) needles
measured over pattern.

ABBREVIATIONS
beg	beginning
k	knit
m1	make
p	purl
psso	pass slipped stitch over
rem	remaining
RS	right side
sl	slip
st st	stocking (stockinette) stitch
sts	stitches
WS	wrong side
yf	yarn forward
yb	yarn back

TECHNIQUES
Sewing up, see page 124
Blocking and pressing, see page 122

KNIT
Sides (make 2)
Using yarn A and 4.5mm (US 7) needles, cast on 79 sts.
ROW 1 (RS): **K1 (yf, sl1, yb, k1) to end.**
ROW 2 (WS): **Purl.**
Change to yarn B.
ROW 3: **K2 (yf, sl1, yb, k1) to last st, k1.**
ROW 4: **Purl.**
The last 4 rows form the pattern.
Keeping pattern correct, dec 1 st at each end of 7th and every following 9th row until 59 sts remain.
Continue straight until work measures 35cm (14in) from cast on edge ending with a RS row. Now working in yarn A only, continue as follows:
NEXT ROW (WS): **Knit. (This creates garter st ridge for turn over at top of bag.)**
NEXT ROW: **Knit.**
NEXT ROW: **Purl.**
Rep last 2 rows once more ending with a WS row.
Cast (bind) off.

Corsage
Make five large petals as follows:
Using yarn C and 3.25mm (US 3) needles, cast on 3 sts.
ROW 1: **K1, p1, k1.**
ROW 2: **K1, m1, k1, m1, k1. (5 sts)**
ROW 3: **K1, p3, k1.**
ROW 4: **K2, m1, k1, m1, k2. (7 sts)**
ROW 5: **K1, p5, k1.**
ROW 6: **K3, m1, k1, m1, k3. (9 sts)**
ROW 7: **K1, p7, k1.**
ROW 8: **K4, m1, k1, m1, k4. (11 sts)**

ROW 9: **K1, p9, k1.**
ROW 10: **K5, m1, k1, m1, k5.** (13 sts)
ROW 11: **K1, p11, k1.**
ROW 12: **K5, sl2, k1, p2sso, k5.** (11 sts)
ROW 13: **K1, p9, k1.**
ROW 14: **K4, sl2, k1, p2sso, k4.** (9 sts)
ROW 15: **K1, p7, k1.**
ROW 16: **K3, sl2, k1, p2sso, k3.** (7 sts)
ROW 17: **K1, p5, k1.**
ROW 18: **K2, sl2, k1, p2sso, k2.** (5 sts)
ROW 19: **K1, p3, k1.**
ROW 20: **K1, sl2, k1, p2sso, k1.** (3 sts)
ROW 21: **K1, p1, k1.**
ROW 22: **Sl2, k1, p2sso. (1 st)**
Fasten off.
Make five small petals as follows:
Using yarn D and 3.25mm (US 3) needles, cast on 3 sts.
ROW 1: **K1, p1, k1.**
ROW 2: **K1, m1, k1, m1, k1. (5 sts)**
ROW 3: **K1, p3, k1.**
ROW 4: **K2, m1, k1, m1, k2. (7 sts)**
ROW 5: **K1, p5, k1.**
ROW 6: **K3, m1, k1, m1, k3. (9 sts)**
ROW 7: **K1, p7, k1.**
ROW 8: **K3, sl2, k1, p2sso, k3. (7 sts)**
ROW 9: **K1, p5, k1.**
ROW 10: **K2, sl2, k1, p2sso, k2.** (5 sts)
ROW 11: **K1, p3, k1.**
ROW 12: **K1, sl2, k1, p2sso, k1.** (3 sts)
ROW 13: **Sl2, k1, p2sso. (1 st)**
Fasten off.

FINISHING

Using mattress stitch, sew together the front and back of the bag by working down one side, across the bottom and up the other side.

Make fabric lining as follows: Using the knitted bag as a template, cut two pieces of lining fabric slightly larger than the knitted pieces plus 1cm (⅜in) at the sides and the bottom for the seam allowance. Sew the two pieces together by working down one side, across the bottom and up the other side. Turn the knitted bag inside out and with the lining fabric also inside out, sew the bottom two corners of the lining to the bottom two corners of the knitted bag. Fold the lining back over the bag and it will now look as if the whole bag has been turned inside out.

Place the wadding in between the knitted bag and the lining fabric and then slip stitch the hems at the top of the bag into place, while securing and covering the top edges of the lining. Turn the bag right side out.

Using the photograph as a guide, attach the handles by sewing neatly into place inside the top of the bag.

Add the corsage to the top left hand corner of the bag, as illustrated on page 10.

True Blue

Never out of your jeans? Combine your everyday wardrobe with this hip and funky tote. This medley of greys and blues can only enhance your denim collection. Large enough to fit real everyday essential items, this style is designed to work for you and your lifestyle needs.

SIZE
39cm × 24cm (15¼in × 9¾in)

MATERIALS
4.5mm (US 7) needles

Yarn
Rowan Summer Tweed
50g (1¾oz) balls
    529 Denim (A)   3

Rowan Kid Classic
50g (1¾oz) balls
    840 Crystal (B)   1

2 pieces, each measuring
50cm × 50cm (20in × 20in) lining
and wadding fabric (approximately)

TENSION (GAUGE)
16 sts and 22 rows to 10cm (4in)
using 4.5mm (US 7) needles
measured over stocking
(stockinette) stitch.

ABBREVIATIONS
beg	beginning
k	knit
k2tog	knit two stiches together
k2togtbl	knit two together through back loop
p	purl
p2tog	purl two stitches together
p2togtbl	purl two stitches together through back loop
psso	pass slipped stitch over
rem	remaining

RS	right side
sl	slip
st st	stocking (stockinette) stitch
sts	stitches
WS	wrong side

TECHNIQUES
Sewing up, see page 124
Blocking and pressing, see page 122

KNIT
Sides (make 2)
Using yarn A and 4.5mm (US 7) needles, cast on 63 sts.
ROW 1 (RS): Knit.
ROW 2 (WS): Purl.
Repeat last 2 rows until work measures 25cm (10in) from cast on edge ending with a WS row.
NEXT ROW (RS): K45, turn and cast (bind) off centre 27 sts and purl to end.
Working on these 18 sts only continue as follows:
NEXT ROW: K to last 3 sts, k2togtbl, k1. (17 sts)
NEXT ROW: P1, p2tog, purl to end. (16 sts)
Repeat last 2 rows until 3 sts remain.
NEXT ROW: Slip 2, k1, p2sso.
Fasten off.
With RS facing, rejoin yarn to remaining 18 sts and continue as follows:

NEXT ROW: K1, k2tog, k to end. (17 sts)
NEXT ROW: P to last 3 sts, p2togtbl, p1. (16 sts)
Repeat last 2 rows until 3 sts remain.
NEXT ROW: Slip 2, k1, p2sso.
Fasten off.

Handle (worked all in one piece)
Using yarn B and 4.5mm (US 7) needles, cast on 15 sts.
ROW 1: Knit.

ROW 2: K1, p13, k1.
Repeat last 2 rows until work measures 150cm (59in) ending with a WS row.
Cast (bind) off.

Flower
Using yarn B and 4.5mm (US 7) needles, cast on 117 sts.
ROW 1: K1, *k2 lift first of these 2 over second, rep from * to end. (59 sts)
ROW 2: P2tog to last st, p1. (30 sts)
Change to yarn A.

ROW 3: **Knit.**

ROW 4: **Purl.**

Do not cast (bind) off. Thread yarn through remaining stitches and pull together.

FINISHING

Using the photograph on the previous page as a guide, sew the flower to the front of the bag at the top left corner.

Position the handle in such a way that there is sufficient left free at either side of the top for the handle. Mark the position of the base on the handle and then using mattress stitch sew the side edges of the base to the cast on edges of the front and back of the bag. Now sew each of the four side seams.

Make fabric lining as follows: NOTE: the bag is only lined up to the cast (bound) off edge of the front and back.

Using the knitted bag as a template, cut out two pieces of lining fabric slightly larger than the front and back pieces plus 1cm (⅜in) at the sides and the bottom for the seam allowance. Do the same for the base and two sides allowing 1cm (⅜in) seam *all the way round* for the side pieces. You will now have five pieces of lining fabric. Sew a 1cm (⅜in) hem across the top edges of all pieces to neaten them up as they will be seen. Sew lining together as you did for the knitted pieces.

Now, turn the knitted bag inside out and with the lining fabric also inside out, sew the bottom four corners of the lining to the bottom four corners of the knitted bag. Keeping the knitted bag inside out, turn the fabric lining back over the

bag. It will now look as if the whole bag has been turned inside out.

Slip stitch the knitted hems at the top of the bag into place, securing and covering the top edges of the lining. Turn the bag right side out.

Tie the two cast (bound) off edges of the handle together in a knot.

to the next level

To add texture to this design, try creating several corsages in various sizes and sewing them in one corner.

Very Berry

In the spotlight – nubby bobbles worked in a variety of textures enhance this very tactile satchel. They also complement the softness of the bag while the choice of colours blends together perfectly. Try your hand at making bobbles.

SIZE
28cm × 27cm (11in × 10¾in)

MATERIALS
4.5mm (US 7) needles

Yarn
Rowan Kid Classic
50g (1¾oz) balls
    847 Cherry (A)   2

Rowan Cotton Glacé
50g (1¾oz) balls
    741 Poppy (B)   1

Rowan Cotton Glacé
50g (1¾oz) balls
    823 Damson (C)   1

Rowan Scottish Tweed DK
50g (1¾oz) balls
    017 Lobster (D)   1

2 pieces, each measuring
43cm × 43cm (17in × 17in) lining
and wadding fabric (approximately)

TENSION (GAUGE)
18 sts and 25 rows to 10cm (4in)
using 4.5mm (US 7) needles
measured over stocking
(stockinette) stitch.

ABBREVIATIONS
beg   beginning
k   knit
p   purl
rem   remaining
RS   right side
sl   slip
st st   stocking (stockinette) stitch
sts   stitches
WS   wrong side

TECHNIQUES
Sewing up, see page 124
Blocking and pressing, see page 122

KNIT
Front
Using yarn A and 4.5mm (US 7)
needles, cast on 51 sts.
ROW 1: **Knit.**
ROW 2: **Purl.**
Repeat last 2 rows twice more
ending with a WS row.
Now work rows 1–61 from the
chart making bobbles as follows:
MB: Knit into the front, back, front,
        and back of next st (4 sts),
        turn p4, turn k4, turn p4, turn
        k4, turn p4, turn sl2, k2tog,
        p2sso.
No longer working from the chart,
continue as follows:
Change to yarn D.
NEXT ROW: **Knit.**
NEXT ROW: **Purl.**
Repeat last 2 rows twice more
times ending with RS row.
NEXT ROW (WS): **Knit.**
Change to yarn A.
NEXT ROW: **Knit.**
NEXT ROW: **Purl.**

Repeat last 2 rows twice more
ending with a ws row.
Cast (bind) off.

Back
Using yarn A and 4.5mm (US 7)
needles, cast on 51 sts.
ROW 1: **Knit.**
ROW 2: **Purl.**
Repeat last 2 rows until work
measures 25cm (9¾in)
from cast on edge
ending with a WS row.
Change to yarn D.
NEXT ROW: **Knit.**
NEXT ROW: **Purl.**

Repeat last 2 rows twice more
times ending with RS row.
NEXT ROW (WS): **Knit.**
Change to yarn A.
NEXT ROW: **Knit.**
NEXT ROW: **Purl.**
Repeat last 2 rows twice more
ending with a WS row.
Cast (bind) off.

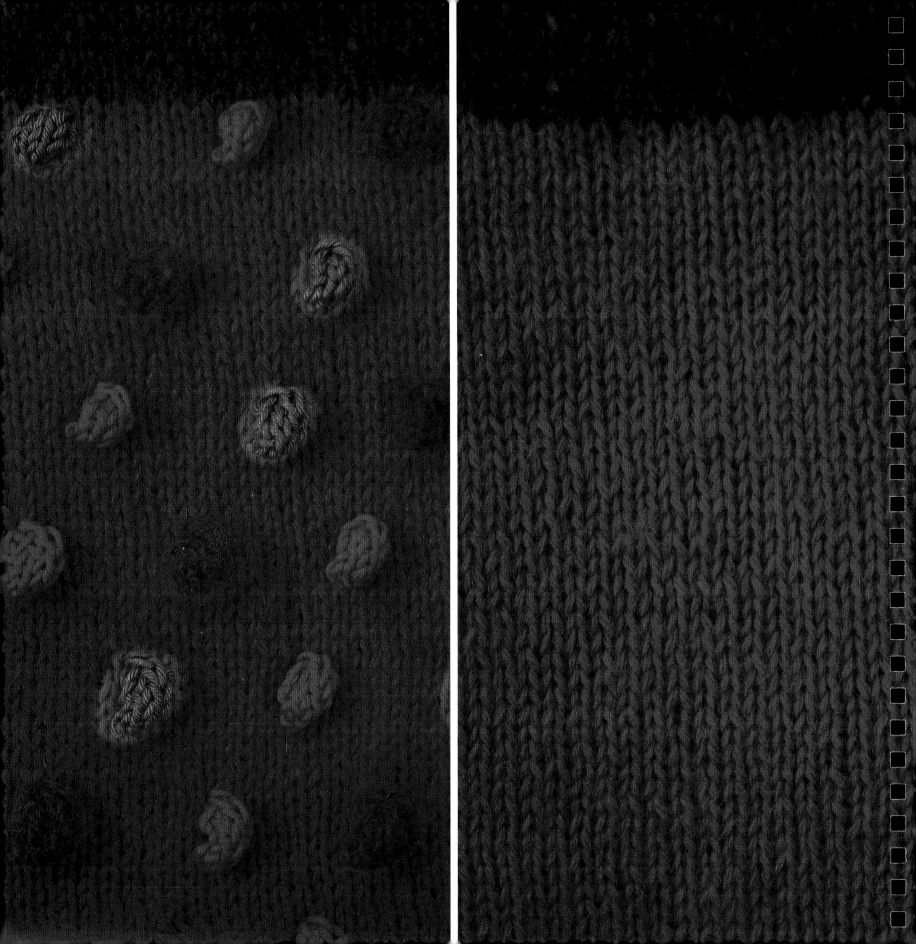

CHART

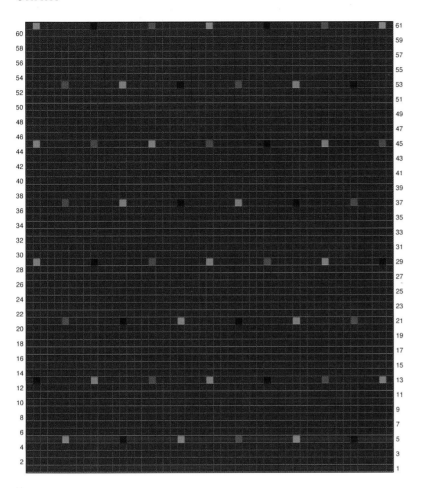

60	61
58	59
56	57
54	55
52	53
50	51
48	49
46	47
44	45
42	43
40	41
38	39
36	37
34	35
32	33
30	31
28	29
26	27
24	25
22	23
20	21
18	19
16	17
14	15
12	13
10	11
8	9
6	7
4	5
2	3
	1

Key
- A (Cherry)
- B (Poppy)
- C (Damson)
- D (Lobster)

Handles (make 2)
Using yarn A and 4.5mm (US 7) needles, cast on 7 sts.

ROW 1: **Knit.**

ROW 2: **K1, p5, k1.**

Repeat last 2 rows until work measures 45cm (17½in) from cast on edge, ending with a WS row. Cast (bind) off.

FINISHING
Using mattress stitch, sew together the front and back of the bag by working down one side, across the bottom and up the other side.

Make fabric lining as follows: Using the knitted bag as a template, cut two pieces of lining fabric slightly larger than the knitted pieces plus 1cm (⅜in) at the sides and the bottom for the seam allowance. Sew the two pieces together by working down one side, across the bottom and up the other side. Turn the knitted bag inside out and with the lining fabric also inside out, sew the bottom two corners of the lining to the bottom two corners of the knitted bag. Fold the lining back over the bag and it will now look as if the whole bag has been turned inside out.

Place the wadding in between the knitted bag and the lining fabric and then slip stitch the hems at the top of the bag into place, at the same time securing and covering the top edges of the lining. Turn the bag right side out.

Sew handles into place inside bag approx. 6cm (2¼in) in from side seams.

Tangerine

A chunky cable pattern offers ample texture and a bright citrus hue delivers maximum appeal. Decorative bamboo handles will make you want to hold on to this one forever. No matter what the occasion, this bag will be a talking point wherever it goes!

SIZE
36cm at widest point × 30cm (14¼in × 12in)

MATERIALS
6mm (US 10) needles

Yarn
Rowan Cotton Rope
50g (1¾oz) balls
061 Squash   5

Bamboo handles (Prym 615101) attached using silver rings (Prym 615130)
2 pieces, each measuring 50cm × 46cm (20in × 18in) lining and wadding fabric (approximately)

TENSION (GAUGE)
15 sts and 20 rows to 10cm (4in) using 6mm (US 10) needles measured over stocking (stockinette) stitch.

ABBREVIATIONS
beg   beginning
C8B   slip next 4 stitches onto cable needle and hold at back of work, knit 4 stitches from left hand needle and then knit the 4 stitches from the cable needle.
k   knit
MB   knit into the front, back, front and back of next st (4 sts), turn p4, turn k4, turn p4, turn k4, turn p4, turn sl2, k2tog, p2sso.
p   purl
rem   remaining
RS   right side
sl   slip
st st stocking (stockinette) stitch
sts   stitches
WS   wrong side

TECHNIQUES
Sewing up, see page 124
Blocking and pressing, see page 122
Cables, see page 121

KNIT
Front
Using 6mm (US 10) needles, cast on 60 sts.
ROW 1 (RS): (P9, k8) to last 9 sts, p9.
ROW 2 (WS): (K9, p8), to last 9 sts, k9.
Repeat last 2 rows once more ending with a WS row.
ROW 5: P4, MB, p4 (k8, p4, MB, p4) to end.
ROW 6: As row 2.
ROW 7: (P9, C8B) to last 9 sts, p9.
ROW 8: As row 2.
ROW 9: As row 1.
ROW 10: As row 2.
Rep rows 5–10 eight more times ending with a WS row AND AT THE SAME TIME decrease 1 st at either side of the cable panels on the 15th and every following 11th row until 36 sts.

Note: you will lose 6 sts on each dec row.
NEXT ROW: Knit.
NEXT ROW: Knit. (This creates garter-stitch ridge for turn over at top of bag.)
NEXT ROW: Knit.
NEXT ROW: Purl.

Repeat last 2 rows once more ending with a WS row.
Cast (bind) off.

Back
Work as for the front, omitting bobbles.

FINISHING

Using mattress stitch, sew together the front and back of the bag by working down one side, across the bottom and up the other side.

Make fabric lining as follows: Using the knitted bag as a template, cut two pieces of lining fabric slightly larger than the knitted pieces plus 1cm (⅜in) at the sides and the bottom for the seam allowance. Sew the two pieces together by working down one side, across the bottom and up the other side. Now, turn the knitted bag inside out and with the lining fabric also inside out, sew the bottom two corners of the lining to the bottom two corners of the knitted bag. Fold the lining back over the bag and it will now look as if the whole bag has been turned inside out.

Place the wadding in between the knitted bag and the lining fabric and then slip stitch the hems at the top of the bag into place, at the same time securing and covering the top edges of the lining. Turn the bag right side out.

Using the photograph as a guide, attach the handles by sewing neatly into place inside the top of the bag.

tangerine bobble

This bag would look great in a rainbow of colours – why not knit yourself a collection?

Frill Seeker

Sumptuous layers of frills are the focus of this ultra-chic design. A gentle alliance of subtle greens pleases the eye while soft tweed, paired with the silk and mohair blend, creates the luxurious effect. The handles can be knitted to your preferred length.

SIZE
37cm × 35cm (14¾in × 14in)

MATERIALS
6.5mm (US 10½) needles
3.75mm (US 5) needles

Yarn
Rowan Felted Tweed
50g (1¾oz) balls
  146 Herb   4

Rowan Kid Silk Haze
50g (1¾oz) balls
  597 Jelly   1
  582 Trance   1
  581 Meadow   1

50cm × 50cm (20in × 20in) lining
and wadding fabric (approximately)
Magnetic snap (Prym 416480)

Yarn combinations as follows:
Yarn A   Rowan Felted Tweed sh.
         Herb (used double)
Yarn B   One strand of Rowan
         Felted Tweed sh. Herb and
         two strands of Kid Silk
         Haze sh. Jelly
Yarn C   One strand of Rowan
         Felted Tweed sh. Herb and
         two strands of Kid Silk
         Haze sh. Trance
Yarn D   One strand of Rowan
         Felted Tweed sh. Herb and
         two strands of Kid Silk
         Haze sh. Meadow

TENSION (GAUGE)
14 sts and 20 rows to 10cm (4in)
using 6.5mm (US 10½) needles
measured over reverse stocking
(stockinette) stitch.

ABBREVIATIONS
beg	beginning
k	knit
p	purl
p2tog	purl two stitches together
rem	remaining
RS	right side
sl	slip
st st	stocking (stockinette) stitch
sts	stitches
WS	wrong side

TECHNIQUES
Sewing up, see page 124
Blocking and pressing, see page 122

KNIT
Sides (make 2)
First frill:
Using yarn combination B and 6.5mm (US 10½) needles, cast on 205 sts.
ROW 1: K1, *k2 lift first of these 2 over second, rep from * to end. (103 sts)
ROW 2: (P2tog) to last st, p1. (52 sts)
Change to a double strand of yarn A.
ROW 3 (RS): Knit.
ROW 4 (WS): Purl.
These two rows form st st.
ROWS 5–6: Repeat rows 3 and 4 once more ending with a WS row. Break off yarn and leave stitches on a holder.

Second frill:
Using yarn combination C, repeat rows 1 and 2 of first section. You now have a second frill.
Slip the stitches of the first section off their holder and onto a spare needle. Place the needle of the second frill in front of the needle holding the first section of knitting with right sides facing. Using two strands of A and a third needle knit together the first stitch on the front needle together with the first stitch on the back needle. Continue in this way until the whole row has been completed and the second frill is attached. Still using a double strand of yarn A, work rows 4 to 6 of the first section.
Break off yarn and leave stitches on a holder.

Third frill:
Using yarn combination D, repeat rows 1 and 2 of first section. You now have a third frill.
Slip the stitches of the second section off their holder and onto a spare needle. Place the needle of the third frill in front of the needle holding the second section of knitting with right sides facing.

Using yarn A and a third needle, knit together the first stitch on the front needle together with the first stitch on the back needle. Continue in this way until the whole row has been completed and the third frill is attached.

Now that all three frills have been attached commence as follows:

Main section:
Change to yarn combination B.
NEXT ROW (WS): Knit.
NEXT ROW: Purl.
These two rows set the reverse stocking (stockinette) stitch pattern.
Repeat the last 2 rows once more ending with a RS row.
Change to yarn combination A.
NEXT ROW (WS): Knit.
NEXT ROW: Purl.
Repeat the last 2 rows until work measures 35cm (14in) from top of first frill ending with a WS row.
Cast (bind) off.

Handles (make 2)
Using yarn combination A and 3.75mm (US 5) needles, cast on 7 sts.
ROW 1: Knit.
ROW 2: K1, p5, k1.
Repeat last 2 rows until work measures 45cm (17½in) from cast on edge, ending with a WS row.
Cast (bind) off.

FINISHING

Using mattress stitch, sew together the front and back of the bag by working down one side, across the bottom and up the other side.

Make fabric lining as follows: Using the knitted bag as a template, cut out two pieces of lining fabric slightly larger than the knitted pieces plus 1cm (⅜in) all the way round for the seam allowance. Sew a 1cm (⅜in) hem across the top edges of both pieces to neaten them up as they will be seen. Sew the two pieces together by working down one side, across the bottom and up the other side.

Now, turn the knitted bag inside out and with the lining fabric also inside out, sew the bottom two corners of the lining to the bottom two corners of the knitted bag. Keeping the knitted bag inside out, turn the fabric lining back over the bag. It will now look as if the whole bag has been turned inside out.

Place the wadding in between the knitted bag and the lining fabric. Position and attach the front and back of the magnetic snap to the two pieces of lining fabric. Slip stitch the lining into place around the top of the bag. Turn the bag the right way out.

Sew handles into place inside bag approx. 12cm (4¾in) in from side seams.

Crimson and Clover

Accented with a stocking stitch hem, this elegantly-shaped, garter-stitched bag is sure to grab the attention it deserves. Embellished with a floral corsage, this timeless design will be a permanent highlight in your collection.

SIZE
25cm × 29cm (10in × 11½in)

MATERIALS
4.5mm (US 7) needles
3.25mm (US 3) needles

Yarn
Rowan All Seasons Cotton
50g (1¾oz) balls
    211 Blackcurrant (A)   4

Rowan Scottish Tweed 4ply
25g (1oz) balls
    013 Claret (B)   1

Rowan Lurex Shimmer
25g (1oz) balls
    331 Claret (C)   1

Rowan Kid Silk Haze
25g (1oz) balls
    583 Blushes (D)   1
    606 Candy Girl (E)   1

4 × silver rings
2 pieces, each measuring
40cm × 46cm (16in × 18in) lining
and wadding fabric (approximately)

TENSION (GAUGE)
18 sts and 25 rows to 10cm (4in)
using 4.5mm (US 7) needles
measured over stocking
(stockinette) stitch.

ABBREVIATIONS
beg	beginning
k	knit
p	purl
psso	pass slipped stitch over
p2tog	purl two stitches together
rem	remaining
RS	right side
sl	slip
st st	stocking (stockinette) stitch
sts	stitches
WS	wrong side

TECHNIQUES
Sewing up, see page 124
Blocking and pressing, see page 122

KNIT
Sides (make 2)
Using yarn A and 4.5mm (US 7) needles, cast on 47 sts.
ROW 1 (RS): **Knit.**
ROW 2 (WS): **Purl.**
ROW 3: **Knit.**
Repeat last 2 rows twice more ending with a RS row.
ROW 8: **Knit.** (This creates garter-stitch ridge for turn over at top of bag.)
ROW 9: **Knit.**
ROW 10: **Purl.**
Repeat last 2 rows eight more times, ending with a WS row.
ROW 27: **Knit.**
Repeat this row until work measures 26cm (10¼in) from garter-stitch ridge, ending with a WS row.
NEXT ROW (DEC): **K2, sl1, k1, psso (k2, sl1, k1, psso) to last 3 sts, k3. (36 sts)**
NEXT ROW: **Purl.**
NEXT ROW: **Knit.**
NEXT ROW: **Purl.**
NEXT ROW: **K2, sl1, k1, psso (k1, sl1, k1, psso) to last 2 sts, k2. (25 sts)**
NEXT ROW: **Purl.**
NEXT ROW: **Knit.**

NEXT ROW: **Purl.**
NEXT ROW: **K1 (sl1, k1, psso) to end. (13 sts)**
NEXT ROW: **Purl.**
NEXT ROW: **K1 (sl1, k1, psso) to end. (7 sts)**
DO NOT cast (bind) off. Thread yarn through remaining stitches and pull together.
Fasten off.

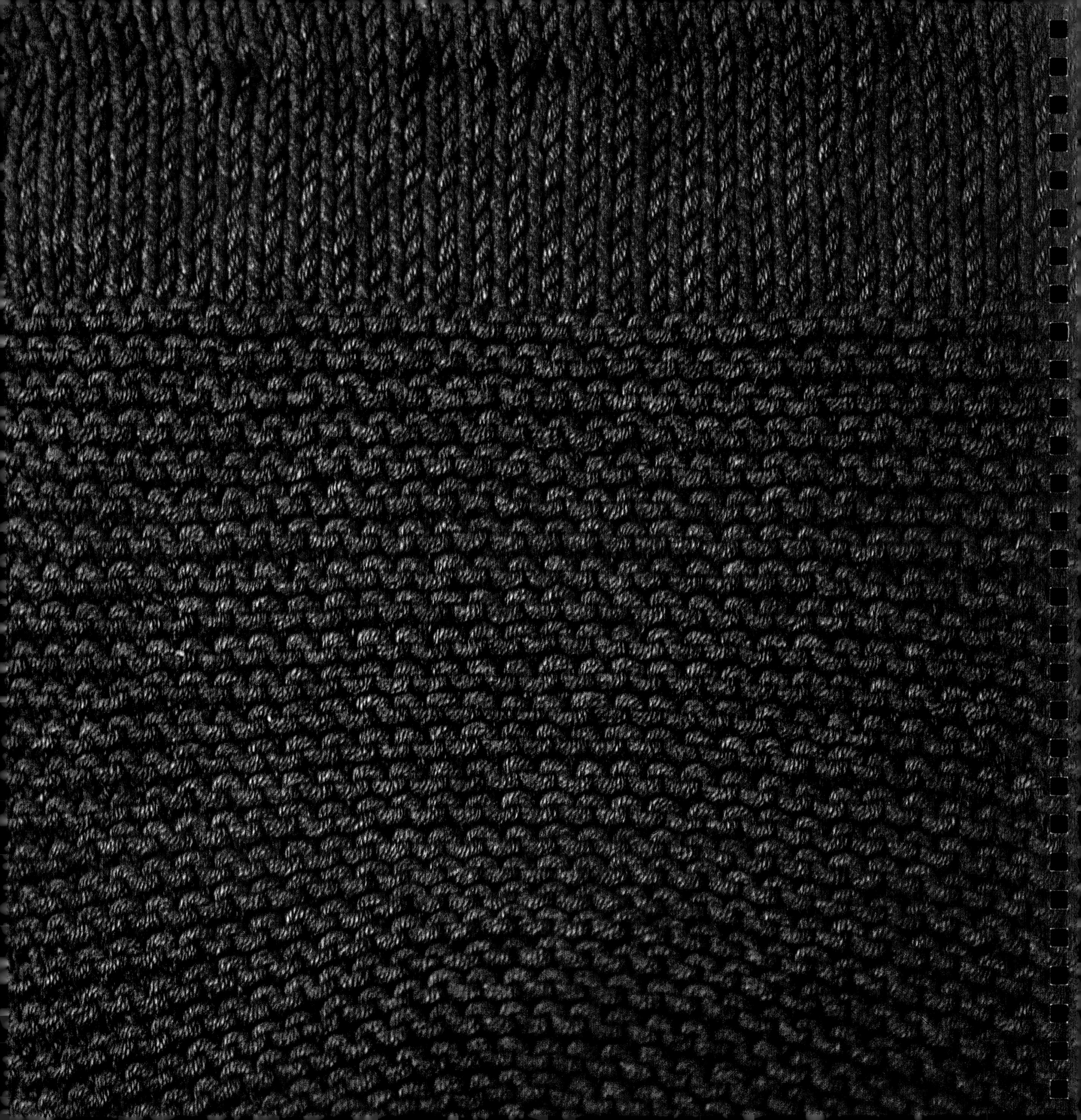

Handles (make 2)

Using yarn A and 4.5mm (US 7) needles, cast on 4 sts.

ROW 1 (RS): **Knit.**

ROW 2 (WS): **K1, p2, k1.**

Repeat last 2 rows once more ending with a WS row.

ROW 5: **Knit.**

ROW 6: **Knit. (This creates garter-stitch fold.)**

ROW 7: **Knit.**

ROW 8: **K1, p2, k1.**

Repeat last 2 rows until work measures 40cm (16in) from cast on edge ending with a RS row.

NEXT ROW (WS): **Knit. (This creates garter-stitch fold.)**

NEXT ROW: **Knit.**

NEXT ROW: **K1, p2, k1.**

Repeat last 2 rows once more ending with a WS row.

Cast (bind) off.

Flowers

Make two flowers as follows:

Using yarn C and 3.25mm (US 3) needles, cast on 93 sts.

Change to yarn B.

ROW 1: **K1, *k2 lift first of these 2 over second, rep from * to end. (47 sts)**

ROW 2: **(P2tog) to last st, p1. (24 sts)**

ROW 3: **Knit.**

ROW 4: **Purl.**

DO NOT cast (bind) off. Thread yarn through remaining stitches and pull together.

Make one flower as follows:

Using yarn E and 3.25mm (US 3) needles, cast on 93 sts.

Change to yarn B.

ROW 1: **K1, *k2 lift first of these 2 over second, rep from * to end. (47 sts)**

ROW 2: **(P2tog) to last st, p1. (24 sts)**

ROW 3: **Knit.**

ROW 4: **Purl.**

DO NOT cast (bind) off. Thread yarn through remaining stitches and pull together.

Make one flower as follows:

Using yarn D and 3.25mm (US 3) needles, cast on 93 sts.

ROW 1: **K1, *k2 lift first of these 2 over second, rep from * to end. (47 sts)**

ROW 2: **(P2tog) to last st, p1. (24 sts)**

ROW 3: **Knit.**

ROW 4: **Purl.**

DO NOT cast (bind) off. Thread yarn through remaining stitches and pull together.

Make one flower as follows:

Using yarn E and 3.25mm (US 3) needles, cast on 93 sts.

ROW 1: **K1, *k2 lift first of these 2 over second, rep from * to end. (47 sts)**

ROW 2: **(P2tog) to last st, p1. (24 sts)**

ROW 3: **Knit.**

ROW 4: **Purl.**

DO NOT cast (bind) off. Thread yarn through remaining stitches and pull together.

FINISHING

Using the photograph on the previous page as a guide, sew the five flowers into place on the front of the bag at the top left corner.

Using mattress stitch, sew together the front and back of the bag by working down one side, across the bottom and up the other side.

Make fabric lining as follows: Using the knitted bag as a template, cut two pieces of lining fabric slightly larger than the knitted pieces plus 1cm (⅜in) at the sides and the bottom for the seam allowance. Sew the two pieces together by working down one side, across the bottom and up the other side. Now, turn the knitted bag inside out and with the lining fabric also inside out, sew the bottom two corners of the lining to the bottom two corners of the knitted bag. Fold the lining back over the bag and it will now look as if the whole bag has been turned inside out.

Place the wadding in between the knitted bag and the lining fabric and then slip stitch the hems at the top of the bag into place, at the same time securing and covering the top edges of the lining. Turn the bag right side out.

Fold each end of the handles round a silver ring using the garter-stitch ridge as the folding row and slip stitch into place. Using the photograph as a guide, sew each ring neatly and securely into place inside the top of the bag.

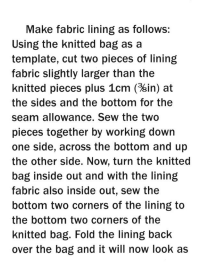

Flutter

A simple, yet pretty, stitch provides the background for a decorative beaded butterfly. Create the wings in your favourite colours and make the body using a whimsical knitted I-cord. Complete the look with sparkling beads.

SIZE
24cm × 26cm (9¾in × 10¼in)

MATERIALS
5.5mm (US 9) needles
3.25mm (US 3) needles
3.25mm (US 3) double-pointed needles

Yarn
Rowan Wool Cotton
50g (1¾oz) balls
   941 Clear (A)   4
   (use double throughout)

Rowan 4ply Cotton
50g (1¾oz) balls
   129 Aegean (B)   1

Rowan Cotton Glacé
50g (1¾oz) balls
   809 Pier (C)   1

Approx. 42 Rowan Beads 01013 (Turquoise)
Acrylic handles (Prym 615104)
2 pieces, each measuring
39cm × 41cm (15in × 16in) lining and wadding fabric (approximately)

TENSION (GAUGE)
16sts and 22 rows to 10cm (4in) using 5.5mm (US 9) needles measured over stocking (stockinette) stitch.

ABBREVIATIONS
beg	beginning
k	knit
m1	make one stitch
p	purl
PB	place bead: yarn forward, slip bead to front of work, sl1 st purlwise, take yarn to back of work. Bead will now be sitting in front of slipped stitch
p2sso	pass two slipped stitches over
rem	remaining
RS	right side
sl	slip
st st	stocking (stockinette) stitch
sts	stitches
WS	wrong side

TECHNIQUES
Sewing up, see page 124
Blocking and pressing, see page 122
Knitting with beads, see page 118

KNIT
Sides (make 2)
Using yarn A and 5.5mm (US 9) needles, cast on 39 sts.
ROW 1: **Knit.**
ROW 2: **Purl.**
ROW 3: **(K1, p1) to last st, k1.**
ROW 4: **Purl.**
ROW 5: **Knit.**
ROW 6: **Purl.**
ROW 7: **K2 (p1, k1) to last 3 sts, p1, k2.**
ROW 8: **Purl.**
Repeat rows 1–8 until work measures 26cm (10¼in) ending with a RS row.
NEXT ROW: **Purl.**
NEXT ROW: **Knit.**
NEXT ROW (WS): **Knit.** (This creates garter-stitch ridge for turn over at top of bag.)
NEXT ROW: **Knit.**
NEXT ROW: **Purl.**
Repeat last 2 rows once more ending with a WS row.
Cast (bind) off.

Butterfly
Wings (make 2)
Using yarn B and size 3.25mm (US 3) needles, cast on 3 sts.
ROW 1: **K1, p1, k1.**
ROW 2: **K1, m1, k1, m1, k1.** (5 sts)
ROW 3: **K1, p3, k1.**
ROW 4: **K2, m1, k1, m1, k2.** (7 sts)
ROW 5: **K1, p5, k1.**
ROW 6: **K3, m1, k1, m1, k3.** (9 sts)
ROW 7: **K1, p7, k1.**
ROW 8: **K4, m1, k1, m1, k4.** (11 sts)
ROW 9: **K1, p9, k1.**
ROW 10: **K5, m1, k1, m1, k5.** (13 sts)
ROW 11: **K1, p11, k1.**

ROW 12: **K6, m1, k1, m1, k6.**
(15 sts)
ROW 13: **K1, p13, k1.**
ROW 14: **K6, sl2, k1, p2sso, k6.**
(13 sts)
ROW 15: **K1, p11, k1.**
ROW 16: **K5, sl2, k1, p2sso, k5.**
(11 sts)
ROW 17: **K1, p9, k1.**
ROW 18: **K4, sl2, k1, p2sso, k4.**
(9 sts)
ROW 19: **K1, p7, k1.**
ROW 20: **K3, sl2, k1, p2sso, k3.**
(7 sts)
ROW 21: **K1, p5, k1.**
ROW 22: **K2, sl2, k1, p2sso, k2.**
(5 sts)
ROW 23: **K1, p3, k1.**
ROW 24: **K1, sl2, k1, p2sso, k1.**
(3 sts)
ROW 25: **K1, p1, k1.**
ROW 26: **Sl2, k1, p2sso. (1 st)**
Fasten off.

Beaded Wings (make 2)
NOTE: thread beads required before cast on.
Using yarn C and size 3.25mm (US 3) needles, cast on 3 sts.
ROW 1: **K1, p1, k1.**
ROW 2: **K1, m1, k1, m1, k1. (5 sts)**
ROW 3: **K1, p3, k1.**
ROW 4: **K1, PB, m1, k1, m1, PB, k1.**
(7 sts)
ROW 5: **K1, p5, k1.**
ROW 6: **K1, PB, k1, m1, k1, m1, k1, PB, k1. (9 sts)**
ROW 7: **K1, p7, k1.**
ROW 8: **K1, PB, k2, m1, k1, m1, k2, PB, k1. (11 sts)**
ROW 9: **K1, p9, k1.**
ROW 10: **K1, PB, k3, m1, k1, m1, k3, PB, k1. (13 sts)**
ROW 11: **K1, p11, k1.**
ROW 12: **K1, PB, k4, m1, k1, m1, k4, PB, k1. (15 sts)**
ROW 13: **K1, p13, k1.**
ROW 14: **K1, PB, k4, sl2, k1, p2sso, k4, PB, k1. (13 sts)**
ROW 15: **K1, p11, k1.**

ROW 16: **K1, PB, k3, sl2, k1, p2sso, k3, PB, k1. (11 sts)**
ROW 17: **K1, p9, k1.**
ROW 18: **K1, PB, k2, sl2, k1, p2sso, k2, PB, k1. (9 sts)**
ROW 19: **K1, p7, k1.**
ROW 20: **K1, PB, k1, sl2, k1, p2sso, k1, PB, k1. (7 sts)**
ROW 21: **K1, p5, k1.**
ROW 22: **K1, PB, sl2, k1, p2sso, PB, k1. (5 sts)**
ROW 23: **K1, p3, k1.**
ROW 24: **K1, sl2, k1, p2sso, k1.**
(3 sts)
ROW 25: **K1, p1, k1.**
ROW 26: **Sl2, k1, p2sso. (1 st)**
Fasten off.

Body
NOTE: The body of the butterfly is made using a technique sometimes known as either a 'knitted cord' or an 'I-cord'. Once you have cast on your stitches, you knit one row. You would now usually turn your needles but to make the cord, **DO NOT TURN.** Instead, slide the stitches to the other end of the double pointed needle ready to be knitted again. The yarn will now be at the left edge of the knitting and so to knit you must pull it tightly across the back of your work and then knit one row. You continue in this way, never turning and always sliding the work to the other end of the double pointed needle and the right side of the work will always be facing you.
Using the technique as described, make the body as follows:
Using 3.25mm (US 3) double pointed needles and yarn B, cast on 4 sts.
ROW 1: **Knit.**
Repeat this row until body is desired length.
Break off yarn, thread through remaining stitches and pull together.

FINISHING
Using mattress stitch, sew together the front and back of the bag by working down one side, across the bottom and up the other side.

Using the photograph on the facing page as a guide and a sewing thread in a matching colour, slip stitch the butterfly wings and body into place neatly and securely. Embroider the antennae using yarn B and chain stitch. Sew a bead to the end of each one.

Make fabric lining as follows: Using the knitted bag as a template, cut two pieces of lining fabric slightly larger than the knitted pieces plus 1cm (⅜in) at the sides and the bottom for the seam allowance. Sew the two pieces together by working down one side, across the bottom and up the other side. Now, turn the knitted bag inside out and with the lining fabric also inside out, sew the bottom two corners of the lining to the bottom two corners of the knitted bag. Fold the lining back over the bag and it will now look as if the whole bag has been turned inside out.

Place the wadding in between the knitted bag and the lining fabric and then slip stitch the hems at the top of the bag into place, at the same time securing and covering the top edges of the lining. Turn the bag right side out.

Using the photograph as a guide, attach the handles by sewing neatly into place inside the top of the bag.

Cinnamon

An autumnal palette, a Fair Isle motif and leather handles work together to lend rustic charm to this enduring bag. The motif is framed by pretty pink beads while the simple shape makes it cool and casual.

SIZE
32cm × 30cm (12½in × 12in)

MATERIALS
4mm (US 6) needles

Yarn
Scottish Tweed DK
50g (1¾oz) balls
    011 Sunset (A)   3

Rowan Wool Cotton
50g (1¾oz) balls
    962 Pumpkin (B)   1

Approx. 80 Rowan Beads 01015
(Pale pink)
Leather handles (Prym 615108)
2 pieces, each measuring
47cm × 44cm (19in × 18in) lining
and wadding fabric (approximately)

TENSION (GAUGE)
20 sts and 28 rows to 10cm (4in)
using 4mm (US 6) needles
measured over stocking
(stockinette) stitch.

ABBREVIATIONS
beg beginning
k   knit
p   purl
PB place bead: yarn forward, slip
     bead to front of work, sl1 st
     purlwise, take yarn to back of
     work. Bead will now be sitting
     in front of slipped stitch.

rem remaining
RS   right side
sl   slip
st st stocking (stockinette) stitch
sts   stitches
WS wrong side

TECHNIQUES
Sewing up, see page 124
Blocking and pressing, see page 122
Fair Isle, see page 117

KNIT
Front
Using yarn A and 4mm (US 6)
needles, cast on 65 sts.
ROW 1 (RS): **K1 (p1, k1) to end.**
Repeat last row until work
measures 20cm (8in) from cast on
edge ending with a WS row.
Now work rows 1–19 from the
chart ending with a WS row.
Change to yarn A.
NEXT ROW: **Knit.**
NEXT ROW: **K1 (p1, k1) to end.**
Repeat last row until work
measures 30cm (12in) from cast
on edge ending with RS row.
NEXT ROW (WS): **Knit.** (This creates
garter-stitch ridge for turn over at
top of bag.)
Change to yarn B.
NEXT ROW: **Knit.**
NEXT ROW: **Purl.**
Repeat last 2 rows three more
times ending with a WS row.
Cast (bind) off.

Back
Using yarn A and 4mm (US 6)
needles, cast on 65 sts.
ROW 1 (RS): **K1 (p1, k1) to end.**
Repeat last row until work
measures 20cm (8in) from cast on
edge ending with a WS row.
Change to yarn B.
NEXT ROW: **Knit.**
NEXT ROW: **Purl.**
Repeat last two rows eight more
times ending with a WS row.
Change to yarn A.
NEXT ROW: **Knit.**

NEXT ROW: **K1 (p1, k1) to end.**
Repeat last row until work
measures 30cm (12in) from cast
on edge ending with RS row.
NEXT ROW (WS): **Knit.** (This creates
garter-stitch ridge for turn over at
top of bag.)
Change to yarn B.
NEXT ROW: **Knit.**
NEXT ROW: **Purl.**
Repeat last 2 rows three more
times ending with a WS row.
Cast (bind) off.

CHART

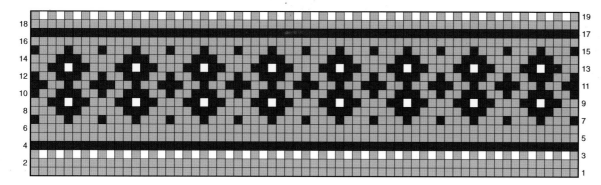

Key
- ■ A (Sunset)
- ▨ B (Pumpkin)
- □ Bead (PB)

FINISHING

Using mattress stitch, sew together the front and back of the bag by working down one side, across the bottom and up the other side.

Make fabric lining as follows: Using the knitted bag as a template, cut two pieces of lining fabric slightly larger than the knitted pieces plus 1cm (⅜in) at the sides and the bottom for the seam allowance. Sew the two pieces together by working down one side, across the bottom and up the other side. Turn the knitted bag inside out and with the lining fabric also inside out, sew the bottom two corners of the lining to the bottom two corners of the knitted bag. Fold the lining back over the bag and it will now look as if the whole bag has been turned inside out.

Place the wadding in between the knitted bag and the lining fabric and then slip stitch the hems at the top of the bag into place, at the same time securing and covering the top edges of the lining. Turn the bag right side out.

Using the photograph as a guide, attach the handles by sewing neatly into place inside the top of the bag.

Purple Haze

Fun and vibrant stripes with dashes of silver work together to create a purple haze. It's a medium sized, practical bag that's wonderful to look at, and even better to wear – you'll be the envy of your friends.

SIZE
28cm × 21cm (11in × 8¼in)

MATERIALS
5.5mm (US 9) needles

Yarn
Rowan Handknit Cotton
50g (1¾oz) balls

314 Decadent (A)	4
305 Lupin (B)	1

Rowan Lurex Shimmer
25g (1oz) balls

333 Pewter (C)	1

Rowan Summer Tweed
50g (1¾oz) balls

539 Vanity (D)	1

Rowan Scottish Tweed 4ply
25g (1oz) balls

016 Thistle (E)	1

2 pieces, each measuring 43cm × 35cm (17in × 14in) lining and wadding fabric (approximately)

TENSION (GAUGE)
13 sts and 16 rows to 10cm (4in) using 5.5mm (US 9) needles measured over stocking (stockinette) stitch.

ABBREVIATIONS

beg	beginning
k	knit
p	purl
rem	remaining
RS	right side
sl	slip
st st	stocking (stockinette) stitch
sts	stitches
WS	wrong side

TECHNIQUES
Sewing up, see page 124
Blocking and pressing, see page 122

KNIT
Sides (make 2)
Using two strands of yarn A held together and 5.5mm (US 9) needles, cast on 37 sts.
ROW 1: Knit.
Repeat this row thirteen more times ending with a WS row.
ROW 15: Knit using two strands of yarn B held together.
ROWS 16–18: Knit using yarns C and D.
ROWS 19–20: Knit using yarns A and E.
ROWS 21–22: Knit using yarns C and D.
ROWS 23–26: Knit using two strands of yarn A held together.
ROW 27: Knit using two strands of yarn B held together.
ROWS 28–29: Knit using yarns C and D.
ROWS 30–31: Knit using yarns A and E.
ROWS 32–34: Knit using two strands of yarn A held together.

ROWS 35–40: Knit using yarns A and E.
ROW 41: Knit using two strands of yarn B held together.
Continue in yarn A only as follows:
ROW 42: Knit.
ROW 43: Knit.
ROW 44: Purl.
Repeat last 2 rows twice more ending with a WS row.
ROW 49: Knit.
ROW 50: Knit. (This creates garter-stitch ridge for turn over at top
of bag.)
ROW 51: Knit.
ROW 52: Purl.
Repeat last 2 rows twice more ending with a WS row.
Cast (bind) off.

Handle
Using yarn A and 5.5mm (US 9) needles, cast on 6 sts.
ROW 1: Knit.
ROW 2: K1, p4, k1.
Repeat last two rows until work measures 70cm (27¾in) from cast on edge ending with a WS row.
Cast (bind) off.

hazy shade of winter

Stripes are a fun and easy way to add visual interest to your bag. Experiment with colours and widths to create some unusual effects.

FINISHING

Using mattress stitch, sew together the front and back of the bag by working down one side, across the bottom and up the other side.

   Make fabric lining as follows: Using the knitted bag as a template, cut two pieces of lining fabric slightly larger than the knitted pieces plus 1cm (⅜in) at the sides and the bottom for the seam allowance. Sew the two pieces together by working down one side, across the bottom and up the other side. Now, turn the knitted bag inside out and with the lining fabric also inside out, sew the bottom two corners of the lining to the bottom two corners of the knitted bag. Fold the lining back over the bag and it will now look as if the whole bag has been turned inside out.

Place the wadding in between the knitted bag and the lining fabric and then slip stitch the hems at the top of the bag into place, at the same time securing and covering the top edges of the lining. Turn the bag right side out.

   Sew handle into place inside the bag at the top of the side seams.

Weekend

Ludo

It's back to school with this bag! The traditional satchel has been thoroughly updated in a bold yarn. Featuring a moss-stitched pocket flap and a large buckle fastening, this easy-going carryall makes a stylish, yet practical, accessory that is red hot.

SIZE
26cm × 32cm (10¼in × 12½in)

MATERIALS
10 mm (US 15) needles

Yarn
Rowan Spray
100g (3¾oz) balls
   04 Sunset   3

Rowan buckle – Red 00362
2 pieces, each measuring
40cm × 48cm (16in × 19in) lining
and wadding fabric (approximately)

TENSION (GAUGE)
9 sts and 11 rows to 10cm (4in)
using 10mm (US 15) needles
measured over stocking
(stockinette) stitch.

ABBREVIATIONS
beg   beginning
k   knit
p   purl
rem   remaining
RS   right side
sl   slip
st st stocking (stockinette) stitch
sts   stitches
WS   wrong side

TECHNIQUES
Sewing up, see page 124
Blocking and pressing, see page 122

KNIT
Sides (make 2)
Using 10mm (US 15) needles, cast on 24 sts.
ROW 1 (RS): **Knit.**
ROW 2 (WS): **Purl.**
Repeat last 2 rows until work measures 32cm (12½in) from cast on edge ending with a RS row.
NEXT ROW: **Knit. (This creates garter-stitch ridge for turn over at top of bag.)**
NEXT ROW: **Knit.**
NEXT ROW: **Purl.**
Repeat last 2 rows once more ending with a WS row.
Cast (bind) off.

Pocket
Using 10mm (US 15) needles, cast on 17 sts.
ROW 1 (RS): **Knit.**
ROW 2 (WS): **Purl.**
Repeat last 2 rows until work measures 25cm (10in) from cast on edge ending with a RS row.
NEXT ROW: **Knit. (This creates garter-stitch ridge for turn over at top of pocket.)**
NEXT ROW: **Knit.**
NEXT ROW: **Purl.**
Cast (bind) off.

Pocket flap
Using 10mm (US 15) needles, cast on 17 sts.
ROW 1 (RS): **K1 (p1, k1) to end.**
Repeat this row until work measures 11cm (4¼in) from cast on edge ending with a RS row.
NEXT ROW: **Knit. (This creates garter-stitch ridge for turn over at edge of flap.)**
NEXT ROW: **Knit.**
NEXT ROW: **Purl.**
Cast (bind) off.

Buckle strip
Using 10mm (US 15) needles, cast on 5 sts.
ROW 1 (RS): **Knit.**
ROW 2 (WS): **Purl.**
Repeat last 2 rows until work measures 15cm (6in) from cast on edge ending with a WS row.
Cast (bind) off.

Handle

Using 10mm (US 15) needles, cast on 5 sts.

ROW 1 (RS): **Knit.**

ROW 2 (WS): **Purl.**

Repeat last 2 rows until work measures 100cm (39¼in) from cast on edge ending with a WS row. Cast (bind) off.

FINISHING

Using mattress stitch, sew together the front and back of the bag by working down one side, across the bottom, and up the other side.

Sew the pocket to the centre of the front of the bag. Position and sew the pocket flap into place above the pocket. Sew the buckle strip to the underneath of the pocket flap and then position and sew the buckle to the pocket accordingly.

Make fabric lining as follows: Using the knitted bag as a template, cut two pieces of lining fabric slightly larger than the knitted pieces plus 1cm (⅜in) at the sides and the bottom for the seam allowance. Sew the two pieces together by working down one side, across the bottom and up the other side. Turn the knitted bag inside out and with the lining fabric also inside out, sew the bottom two corners of the lining to the bottom two corners of the knitted bag. Fold the lining back over the bag and it will now look as if the whole bag has been turned inside out.

Place the wadding in between the knitted bag and the lining fabric and then slip stitch the hems at the top of the bag into place, at the same time securing and covering the top edges of the lining. Turn the bag right side out.

Sew handle into place inside the bag at the top of the side seams.

easy perfection

If you're looking for a first-time project, this accessory makes a great beginner project. Knitted in easy stockining stitch with chunky yarn and big needles, Ludo knits in a flash.

Daffodil

Enhance an A-line shape with a fantastic metallic print yarn and this sunny springtime bag is sure to be a perennial favourite. Large wooden handles complement the overall look – and will complement your wardrobe too!

SIZE
42cm × 29cm (16¼in × 11½in)

MATERIALS
7mm (US 10½) needles
8mm (US 11) needles

Yarn
Rowan Glimmer Print
50g (1¾oz) balls
03 Faded Gold   7

Bamboo bag handles (Rowan 2075000-00402)
2 pieces, each measuring 57cm × 46cm (23in × 18in) lining and wadding fabric (approximately)
Press stud

TENSION (GAUGE)
13 sts and 18 rows to 10cm (4in) using 7mm (US 10½) needles measured over stocking (stockinette) stitch

ABBREVIATIONS
beg	beginning
k	knit
k2tog	knit two stitches together
p	purl
rem	remaining
RS	right side
sl	slip
st st	stocking (stockinette) stitch
sts	stitches
WS	wrong side

TECHNIQUES
Sewing up, see page 124
Blocking and pressing, see page 122

KNIT
Sides (make 2)
Using 7mm (US 10½) needles, cast on 55 sts.
ROW 1 (RS): **Knit.**
ROW 2 (WS): **Purl.**
Repeat last 2 rows five more times ending with a WS row.
ROW 13: **K2tog, knit to last 2sts, k2tog. (53 sts)**
ROW 14: **Purl.**
ROW 15: **Knit.**
ROW 16: **Purl.**
ROW 17: **Knit.**
ROW 18: **Purl.**
ROW 19: **K2tog, knit to last 2sts, k2tog. (51 sts)**
Repeat rows 14–19 until 43 sts remain ending with a RS row.
ROW 26: **Purl.**
ROW 27: **Knit.**
ROW 28: **Purl.**
ROW 29: **K2tog, knit to last 2sts, k2tog. (39 sts)**
ROW 30: **Purl.**
ROW 31: **K2tog, knit to last 2sts, k2tog. (37 sts)**
ROW 32: **Knit. (This creates garter-stitch ridge for turn over at top of bag.)**
ROW 33: **Knit.**
ROW 34: **Purl.**

Repeat last 2 rows twice more ending with a WS row.
Cast (bind) off.

Fastening strip
Using US 11 (8mm) needles. Cast on 9 sts.
ROW 1 (RS): **Knit.**
ROW 2 (WS): **K1, purl 7, k1.**
Repeat last 2 rows until work measures 25cm (10in) from cast on edge ending with a WS row.
Cast (bind) off.

FINISHING

Using mattress stitch, sew together the front and back of the bag, leaving a gap of 8cm (3¼in) at the top of each side, by working down one side, across the bottom and up the other side.

Make fabric lining as follows: Using the knitted bag as a template, cut two pieces of lining fabric slightly larger than the knitted pieces plus 1cm (⅜in) at the sides and the bottom for the seam allowance. Sew the two pieces together, leaving a gap of 8cm (3¼in) at the top of each side, by working down one side, across the bottom and up the other side. Now, turn the knitted bag inside out and with the lining fabric also inside out, sew the bottom two corners of the lining to the bottom two corners of the knitted bag. It will now look as if the whole bag has been turned inside out.

Place the wadding in between the knitted bag and the lining fabric. Slip stitch the hems at the top of the bag into place, trapping the bars of the bamboo handles and covering the top edges of the lining. Turn the bag the right way out.

For a neat finish, you may want to slip stitch the fabric lining to the inside of the bag along the 8cm (3¼in) gap at the top of each side as this will be visible.

Using the photograph as a guide, sew a press stud to the bag and the fastening strip and then slip stitch the strip into place.

Waffle

A play on the traditional 'string' bag, this vintage-inspired version uses a lining to create a more structured look that's timeless without seeming conventional. A chunky twisted cord, which acts as a drawstring, accentuates the shape.

SIZE
50cm × 32cm (19¾in × 12½in)

MATERIALS
12mm (US 17) needles

Yarn
Rowan Cotton Braid
50g (1¾oz) balls
    358 Cezanne (A)   4

Rowan Handknit Cotton
50g (1¾oz) balls
    205 Linen (B)   1

4 pieces of lining and 2 pieces of wadding fabric, each measuring 65cm × 48cm (26in × 19in)

TENSION (GAUGE)
8½ sts and 10 rows to 10cm (4in) using 12mm (US 17) needles measured over stocking (stockinette) stitch.

ABBREVIATIONS
beg	beginning
k	knit
k2tog	knit two stitches together
k3tog	knit three stitches together
p	purl
rem	remaining
RS	right side
sl	slip
st st	stocking (stockinette) stitch
sts	stitches
WS	wrong side
yf	yarn forward

TECHNIQUES
Sewing up, see page 124
Blocking and pressing, see page 122

KNIT
Sides (make 2)
Using 12mm (US 17) needles, cast on 35 sts.
ROW 1: **Knit.**
ROW 2: **Purl.**
ROW 3: **Knit.**
ROW 4: **Knit.**
ROW 5: **Knit.**
ROW 6: **Purl.**
ROW 7: **K1 (yf, k2tog) to end.**
ROW 8: **Purl.**
Repeat last 2 rows until work measures 22cm (8½in) from garter-stitch ridge ending with a WS row.
ROW 11: **Knit.**
ROW 12: **Purl.**
ROW 13: **K2, k3tog (k4, k3tog) to last 2sts, k2. (25 sts)**
ROW 14: **Purl.**
ROW 15: **K2, k3tog (k3, k3tog) to last 2sts, k2. (17 sts)**
ROW 16: **Purl.**
Cast (bind) off.

Handle – twisted cord
Make a twisted cord using yarn A as follows:

Cut 9 lengths of yarn A approx. 200cm (79in) long. Take the nine lengths of yarn and secure at each end with knots. Ask someone to help you and give her/him one end of the yarn while you hold the other. With the yarn outstretched, each end needs to be twisted in opposite directions until it shows signs of twisting back on itself. Now bring the two ends of the cord together and hold tightly allowing the two halves to twist together. Smooth out any bumps by running your fingers up and down the cord and tie a knot to secure. You will now have a twisted cord approximately 90cm (35¼in) long.

Drawstring fastening
Make a twisted cord using yarn B as follows:
Cut 6 lengths of yarn B approx. 300cm (120in) long. Take the six

lengths of yarn and secure at each end with knots. Ask someone to help you and give her/him one end of the yarn while you hold the other. With the yarn outstretched, each end needs to be twisted in opposite directions until it shows signs of twisting back on itself. Bring the two ends of the cord together and hold tightly allowing the two halves to twist together. Smooth out any bumps by running your fingers up and down the cord and tie a knot to secure. You will now have a twisted cord approximately 120cm (47¼in) long.

FINISHING

Using mattress stitch, sew together the front and back of the bag, working down one side, across the bottom and up the other side.

Make fabric lining as follows: Using the knitted bag as a template, cut four pieces of lining fabric slightly larger than the knitted pieces plus 1cm (⅜in) at the sides and the bottom for the seam allowance. Place a piece of wadding between two of the pieces of fabric and sew these together by working all the way round the edge. Repeat with the other two pieces of fabric and the remaining piece of wadding. You now have two pieces of padded lining fabric. Sew these two pieces together by working down one side, across the bottom and up the other side. Turn the knitted bag inside out and with the lining fabric turned the right way out, sew the bottom two corners of the lining to the bottom two corners of the knitted bag. Fold the lining back over the bag and it will

now look as if the whole bag has been turned inside out. Using the photograph as a guide, thread the drawstring through the bag approx. 10cm (4in) down from the top.

Slip stitch the hems at the top of the bag into place, at the same time securing and covering the top edges of the lining. Turn the bag right side out.

Sew handle into place inside the bag at the top of the side seams.

Whirl

Whirlwind romances? This detailed accessory deserves your attention. A round bag worked in a plain stitch is the backdrop to an all-over pattern of embroidery. Decorated with multicoloured swirls, it's not short of colour or texture. Go on and spiral out of control!

SIZE
40cm at widest point × 20cm
(16in × 8in)

MATERIALS
5.5mm (US 9) needles

Yarn
Rowan Wool Cotton
50g (1¾oz) balls
    959 Bilberry Fool (A)   3
    (use double throughout)

Rowan 4ply Cotton
50g (1¾oz) balls
    120 Orchid (B)   1
    130 Ardour (C)   1

Rowan Wool Cotton
50g (1¾oz) balls
    952 Hiss (D)   1

2 pieces, each measuring
68cm × 37cm (27in × 15in) lining
and wadding fabric (approximately)
Magnetic snap (Prym 416480)

TENSION (GAUGE)
14 sts and 20 rows to 10cm (4in)
using 5.5mm (US 9) needles
measured over stocking
(stockinette) stitch.

ABBREVIATIONS
beg   beginning
k   knit
k2tog   knit two stitches together
m1   make one stitch
p   purl
rem   remaining
RS   right side
sl   slip
st st   stocking (stockinette) stitch
sts   stitches
WS   wrong side

TECHNIQUES
Sewing up, see page 124
Blocking and pressing, see page
122
Embroidery (chain stitch), see page
122

KNIT
Sides (make 2)
Using yarn A and 5.5mm (US 9)
needles, cast on 45 sts.
ROW 1 (RS): **Knit.**
ROW 2 (WS): **Purl.**
ROW 3: **Knit.**
Repeat last 2 rows once more
ending with a RS row.
ROW 6: **Knit.** (This creates
garter-stitch ridge for turn over at
top of bag.)
ROW 7: **Knit.**
ROW 8: **Purl.**
Repeat last 2 rows once more,
ending with a WS row.
Place markers on the 5th, 14th,
23rd, 32nd and 41st stitches. You
should have five marked stitches in
total.

ROW 11 (INC ROW): **K4, m1, k marked
st, m1 (k8, m1, k marked st, m1) to
last 4 sts, k4. (55 sts)**
ROW 12: **Purl.**
ROW 13: **Knit.**
ROW 14: **Purl.**
Repeat last two rows twice more,
ending with a WS row.
ROW 19 (INC ROW): **K5, m1, k marked
st, m1 (k10, m1, k marked st, m1)
to last 5 sts, k5. (65 sts)**
ROW 20: **Purl.**
ROW 21: **Knit.**
ROW 22: **Purl.**
Repeat last two rows twice more,
ending with a WS row.
ROW 27 (INC ROW): **K6, m1, k marked
st, m1 (k12, m1, k marked st, m1)
to last 6 sts, k6. (75 sts)**
ROW 28: **Purl.**
ROW 29: **Knit.**
ROW 30: **Purl.**
Repeat last two rows once more,
ending with a WS row.
ROW 31 (DEC ROW): **K5, k2tog, k
marked st, k2tog (k10, k2tog, k
marked st, k2tog) to last 5 sts, K5.
(65 sts)**
ROW 32: **Purl.**
ROW 33: **Knit.**

ROW 34: **Purl.**
Repeat last two rows once more,
ending with a WS row.
ROW 37 (DEC ROW): **K4, k2tog, k
marked st, k2tog (k8, k2tog, k
marked st, k2tog) to last 4 sts, k4.
(55 sts)**
ROW 38: **Purl.**
ROW 39: **Knit.**
ROW 40: **Purl.**
ROW 41 (DEC ROW): **K3, k2tog, k
marked st, k2tog (k6, k2tog, k
marked st, k2tog) to last 3 sts, k3.
(45 sts)**
ROW 42: **Purl.**
ROW 43 (DEC ROW): **K2, k2tog, k
marked st, k2tog (k4, k2tog, k
marked st, k2tog) to last 2sts, k2.
(35 sts)**
ROW 44: **Purl.**
ROW 45 (DEC ROW): **K1, k2tog, k
marked st, k2tog (k2, k2tog, k
marked st, k2tog) to last 1st, k1.
(25 sts)**
ROW 46: **Purl.**
Cast (bind) off.

Handles (make 2)
Using yarn A and 5½mm (US 9)
needles, cast on 5 sts.
ROW 1: **Knit.**

swirl away

Motifs are a great way to liven up an otherwise simple bag.
Chain stitch patterns are fun to make and lend themselves well
to eye-catching graphic designs.

ROW 2: **K1, p3, k1.**
Repeat last 2 rows until work measures 14in (35cm) from cast on edge ending with a WS row. Bind (cast) off.

FINISHING

Using mattress stitch sew together the front and back of the bag by working down one side, across the bottom and up the other side.

Using the photograph as a guide, embroider spirals to the front and back of the bag using chain stitch in yarns B, C and D. Fasten and attach the front and back of the magnetic strap to the knitted hems.

Make fabric lining as follows:
Using the knitted bag as a template, cut two pieces of lining fabric slightly larger than the knitted pieces plus 1cm (⅜in) at the sides and the bottom for the seam allowance. Sew the two pieces together by working down one side, across the bottom and up the other side. Now, turn the knitted bag inside out and with the lining fabric also inside out, sew the bottom two corners of the lining to the bottom two corners of the knitted bag. Fold the lining back over the bag and it will now look as if the whole bag has been turned inside out.

Place the wadding in between the knitted bag and the lining fabric and then slip stitch the hems at the top of the bag into place, at the same time securing and covering the top edges of the lining. Turn the bag right side out.
Sew handles into place inside bag approx. 7cm (2¾in) in from side seams.

Daydreamer

The trellis pattern is smocked using a lightweight cotton and the large wooden handles add extra structure to the bag. I have used a cotton in a similar shade, but why not try using a contrasting colour instead? The results may impress you!

SIZE
40cm × 33cm (16in × 13in)

MATERIALS
15mm (US 19) needles

Yarn
Rowan Big Wool Fusion
100g (3½oz) balls
01 Source (A)   3

4ply Cotton
50g (1¾oz) balls
129 Aegean (B)   1

Bamboo Bag handles
(Rowan Z075000-00402)
2 pieces, each measuring
55cm × 48cm (22in × 19in) lining
and wadding fabric (approximately)

TENSION (GAUGE)
9 sts and 12 rows to 10cm (4in)
using yarn A and 15mm (US 19)
needles measured over pattern.

ABBREVIATIONS
beg   beginning
k   knit
p   purl
rem   remaining
RS   right side
sl   slip
st st stocking (stockinette) stitch
sts   stitches
WS   wrong side

TECHNIQUES
Sewing up, see page 124
Blocking and pressing, see page 122

KNIT
Sides (make 2)
Using yarn A and 15mm (US 19) needles, cast on 47 sts.
ROW 1 (RS): P1, k1 (p3, k1) to last st, p1.
ROW 2 (WS): K1, p1 (k3, p1) to last st, k1.
Repeat last 2 rows fourteen more times ending with a WS row.
NEXT ROW (RS): Cast (bind) off 8 sts, patt to end.
NEXT ROW (WS): Cast (bind) off 8 sts, knit to end. (This creates garter-stitch ridge for turn over at top.)
NEXT ROW: Knit.
NEXT ROW: Purl.
Repeat last 2 rows once more ending with a WS row.
Cast (bind) off.

Smocking
Using a large darning needle and yarn B, sew ribs together to create smocked pattern as follows:
Front
Starting at the top right corner, sew first two ribs together. Taking the yarn behind the work, bring the needle out next to the second rib, three rows down. Sew the second and third ribs together. Take the yarn back behind the work and bring the needle back out next to

dream, dream, dream

This woolly carryall makes such a practical everyday bag as it can hold everything from keys to makeup to my favourite magazines and books. These handles lend a warm and natural feel to the design, but they can easily be replaced with another style if you prefer.

the third rib on the upper row. Sew the third and fourth ribs together. Continue in this way sewing together alternate pairs of ribs on each row. Repeat these two smocking rows until the whole of the front has been smocked.

Back
Repeat the smocking technique as described for the front.

FINISHING

Using mattress stitch, sew together the front and back of the bag, leaving a gap of 8cm (3½in) at the top of each side, by working down one side, across the bottom and up the other side.

Make fabric lining as follows: Using the knitted bag as a template, cut two pieces of lining fabric slightly larger than the knitted pieces plus 1cm (⅜in) at the sides and the bottom for the seam allowance. Sew the two pieces together, leaving a gap of 8cm (3¼in) at the top of each side, by working down one side, across the bottom and up the other side. Now, turn the knitted bag inside out and with the lining fabric also inside out, sew the bottom two corners of the lining to the bottom two corners of the knitted bag. Fold the lining back over the bag and it will now look as if the whole bag has been turned inside out.

Place the wadding in between the knitted bag and the lining fabric. Slip stitch the hems at the top of the bag into place, trapping the bars of the bamboo handles and covering the top edges of the lining. Turn the bag right side out.

For a neat finish you may want to slip stitch the fabric lining to the inside of the bag along the 8cm (3¼in) gap at the top of each side as this will be visible.

Orchard

Short on time, but not on taste? This quick-to-knit bag makes an ideal project for a beginner knitter. The flower on the cute bag charm allows you to try some simple shaping while creating an eye-catching accent with beads and twisted cords.

SIZE
41cm × 35cm (16¼in × 14in)

MATERIALS
12mm (US 17) needles
3.25mm (US 3) needles

Yarn
Rowan Big Wool
100g (1¾oz) balls
    037 Zing (A)   3

4ply Cotton
50g (1¾oz) balls
    133 Cheeky (B)   1

Kid Silk Haze
25g (1oz) balls
    606 Candy Girl (C)   1

Snap hook (Prym 417 900)
Approx. 92 Rowan Beads 01015 (Pale pink)
Approx. 17 Large pink pony beads
2 pieces, each measuring 57cm × 50cm (23in × 20in) lining and wadding fabric (approximately)

TENSION (GAUGE)
8 sts and 12 rows to 10cm (4in) using yarn A and 12mm (US 17) needles measured over stocking (stockinette) stitch.

ABBREVIATIONS
beg	beginning
k	knit
p	purl
p2tog	purl two stitches together
rem	remaining
RS	right side
sl	slip
st st	stocking (stockinette) stitch
sts	stitches
WS	wrong side

TECHNIQUES
Sewing up, see page 124
Blocking and pressing, see page 122

KNIT
Sides (make 2)
Using yarn A and 12mm (US 17) needles, cast on 33 sts.
ROW 1 (RS): **Knit.**
ROW 2 (WS): **K1 (p1, k1) to end.**
Repeat last 2 rows until work measures 35cm (14in) from cast on edge ending with a RS row.
NEXT ROW (WS): **Knit. (This creates garter-stitch ridge for turn over at top of bag.)**
NEXT ROW: **Knit.**
NEXT ROW: **Purl.**
Repeat last 2 rows once more ending with a WS row.
Cast (bind) off.

Handle (make 2)
Using yarn A and 12mm (US 17) needles, cast on 5 sts.
ROW 1: **Knit.**
ROW 2: **K1, p3, k1.**
Repeat last 2 rows until work measures 55cm (21¾in) from cast on edge ending with a WS row.
Cast (bind) off.

Bag Charm
Flower
Using yarn C and 3.25mm (US 3) needles, cast on 93 sts.
Change to yarn B.

ROW 1: **K1, *k2 lift first of these 2 over second, rep from * to end. (47sts)**
ROW 2: **(P2tog) to last st, p1. (24sts)**
ROW 3: **Knit.**
ROW 4: **Purl.**
DO NOT cast (bind) off. Thread yarn through remaining stitches and pull together.

Stem (long)
Using yarn C and 3.25mm (US 3) needles, cast on 43 sts.
Cast (bind) off.

Stem (short)
Using yarn C and 3.25mm (US 3) needles, cast on 19 sts.
Cast (bind) off.

Twisted cord
Cut 2 lengths of yarn A approx. 33cm (13in) long. Take the two lengths of yarn and secure at each end with knots. Ask someone to help you and give her/him one end of the yarn while you hold the other. With the yarn outstretched, each end needs to be twisted in opposite directions until it shows signs of twisting back on itself. Now bring the two ends of the cord together and hold tightly allowing the two halves to twist together. Smooth out any bumps by running your fingers up and down the cord and tie a knot to secure. You will now have a twisted cord approximately 13cm (5¼in) long.

Beaded tassels
Thread 55 of the smaller pink beads onto a length of yarn B and secure at the end with a knot. Repeat this again but this time using the remaining 37 beads.

Thread the larger beads onto a piece of yarn A and secure at the end with a knot.

FINISHING
Using mattress stitch, sew together the front and back of the bag by working down one side, across the bottom and up the other side.

Make fabric lining as follows: Using the knitted bag as a template, cut two pieces of lining fabric slightly larger than the knitted pieces plus 1cm (⅜in) at the sides and the bottom for the seam allowance. Sew the two pieces together by working down one side, across the bottom and up the other side. Now, turn the knitted bag inside out and with the lining fabric also inside out, sew the bottom two corners of the lining to the bottom two corners of the knitted bag. Fold the lining back over the bag and it will now look as if the whole bag has been turned inside out.

Place the wadding in between the knitted bag and the lining fabric and then slip stitch the hems at the top of the bag into place, at the same time securing and covering the top edges of the lining. Turn the bag right side out.

Sew handles into place inside bag approx. 9cm (3½in) in from side seams and sew a press stud fastening into place at top centre of the bag if desired.

To make the bag charm, use the flower as your starting point. Sew the two stems and the twisted cord neatly and securely to the back of the flower. Now, also sew the longest beaded tassel and the

beaded tassel which uses the larger beads into place. Take the shorter beaded tassel and fold in half sewing both ends into place at the back of the flower.

To attach the charm to the snap hook, make a short twisted cord as

described earlier using yarn B. Use this twisted cord to hang the charm from the hook.

Hang the charm from the base of the handle using the photograph on page 68 as a guide.

Blancmange

Pretty in pink, this candy-coloured tote has a great shape that is accentuated by the double drawstring fastening. Carefree pompoms in various sizes are a quirky addition.

SIZE

45cm at widest point × 29cm
(17½in × 11½in)

MATERIALS

8mm (US 11) needles

Yarn
Rowan Holiday
50g (1¾oz) balls
  033 Sea Pink (A)   6

Rowan Handknit Cotton
50g (1¾oz) balls
  303 Sugar (B)   1
  313 Slick (C)   1

2 pieces, each measuring
57cm × 50cm (23in × 20in) lining
and wadding fabric (approximately)
Magnetic snap (Prym 416480)

TENSION (GAUGE)

12 sts and 16 rows to 10cm (4in)
using 8mm (US 11) needles
measured over stocking
(stockinette) stitch.

ABBREVIATIONS

beg	beginning
k	knit
k2tog	knit two stitches together
m1	make one stitch
p	purl
rem	remaining
RS	right side
sl	slip

st st	stocking (stockinette) stitch
sts	stitches
WS	wrong side
yf	yarn forward

TECHNIQUES

Sewing up, see page 124
Blocking and pressing, see page 125

KNIT

Sides (make 2)

Using yarn A and 8mm (US 11)
needles, cast on 46 sts.
ROW 1 (RS): **Knit.**
ROW 2 (WS): **Purl.**
ROW 3: **Knit.**
Repeat last 2 rows once more
ending with a RS row.
ROW 6: **Knit. (This creates
garter-stitch ridge for turn over at
top of bag.)**
ROW 7: **Knit.**
ROW 8: **Purl.**
Repeat last 2 rows four more
times, ending with a WS row.
ROW 17 (EYELET ROW): **K2, yf, k2tog
(k6, yf, k2tog) to last 2 sts, k to
end.**
ROW 18: **Purl.**
ROW 19: **Knit.**
ROW 20: **Purl. (Dec 1 stitch in centre
of this row.) (45 sts)**
ROW 21: **Knit.**
ROW 22: **Purl.**
Place markers on the 5th, 14th,
23rd, 32nd and 41st stitches. You
should have five marked stitches in
total.

ROW 23 (INC ROW): **K4, m1, k marked
st, m1 (k8, m1, k marked st, m1) to
last 4 sts, K4. (55 sts)**
ROW 24: **Purl.**
ROW 25: **Knit.**
ROW 26: **Purl.**
ROW 27: **Knit.**
ROW 28: **Purl.**
ROW 29 (INC ROW): **K5, m1, k marked
st, m1 (k10, m1, k marked st, m1)
to last 5 sts, k5. (65 sts)**
ROW 30: **Purl.**
ROW 31: **Knit.**
ROW 32: **Purl.**
ROW 33: **Knit.**
ROW 34: **Purl.**
ROW 35 (INC ROW): **K6, m1, k marked
st, m1 (k12, m1, k marked st, m1)
to last 6 sts, k6. (75 sts)**

ROW 36: **Purl.**
ROW 37: **Knit.**
ROW 38: **Purl.**
ROW 39: **Knit.**
ROW 40: **Purl.**
ROW 41 (DEC ROW): **K5, k2tog, k
marked st, k2tog (k10, k2tog, k
marked st, k2tog) to last 5 sts, K5.
(65 sts)**
ROW 42: **Purl.**
ROW 43: **Knit.**
ROW 44: **Purl.**
ROW 45 (DEC ROW): **K4, k2tog, k
marked st, k2tog (k8, k2tog, k
marked st, k2tog) to last 4 sts, k4.
(55 sts)**
ROW 46: **Purl.**
ROW 47: **Knit.**

ROW 48: **Purl.**

ROW 49 (DEC ROW): **K3, k2tog, k marked st, k2tog (k6, k2tog, k marked st, k2tog) to last 3sts, k3. (45 sts)**

ROW 50: **Purl.**

ROW 51: **Knit.**

ROW 52: **Purl.**

ROW 53 (DEC ROW): **K2, k2tog, k marked st, k2tog (k4, k2tog, k marked st, k2tog) to last 2sts, k2. (35 sts)**

ROW 54: **Purl.**

ROW 55: **K1, k2tog, k marked st, k2tog (k2, k2tog, k marked st, k2tog) to last st, k1. (25 sts)**
Cast (bind) off.

Handle

Using yarn A and 8mm (US 11) needles, cast on 7 sts.

ROW 1: **Knit.**

ROW 2: **K1, p5, k1.**

Repeat last 2 rows until work measures 65cm (25¾in) from cast on edge, ending with a WS row. Cast (bind) off.

Pompoms

Make one small pompom using yarn B as follows:
Cut two circles of card approx. 2cm (1in) in diameter. Cut a hole in the centre of each approx. 1cm (½in) in diameter. Wind the yarn around the outside of the two circles of card until the hole in the centre is almost filled in. Next, cut slowly and carefully round the edges of the two pieces of card until all the yarn has been cut. Carefully ease the pieces of card apart, but BEFORE taking them off completely, tie a piece of yarn in a secure knot around the centre of the pompom to hold it together. Now remove the card.
Make one medium pompom using yarn C as follows:
Cut two circles of card approx. 3.5cm (1½in) in diameter. Cut a hole in the centre of each approx. 1.5cm (¾in) in diameter. Wind the

yarn around the outside of the two circles of card until the hole in the centre is almost filled in. Next, cut slowly and carefully round the edges of the two pieces of card until all the yarn has been cut. Carefully ease the pieces of card apart, but BEFORE taking them off completely, tie a piece of yarn in a secure knot around the centre of the pompom to hold it together. Now remove the card.
Make one large pompom in yarn B and one large pompom in yarn C as follows:
Cut two circles of card approx. 5.5cm (2¼in) in diameter. Cut a hole in the centre of each approx. 3cm (1¼in) in diameter. Wind the yarn around the outside of the two circles of card until the hole in the centre is almost filled in. Next, cut slowly and carefully round the edges of the two pieces of card until all the yarn has been cut. Carefully ease the pieces of card apart, but BEFORE taking them off completely, tie a piece of yarn in a secure knot around the centre of the pompom to hold it together. Now remove the card.

Twisted cords

Make one twisted cord in yarn B and one in yarn C as follows:
Cut 3 lengths of yarn A approx. 230cm (91in) long. Take the three lengths of yarn and secure at each end with knots. Ask someone to help you and give her/him one end of the yarn while you hold the other. With the yarn outstretched, each end needs to be twisted in opposite directions until it shows signs of twisting back on itself. Now bring the two ends of the cord together and hold tightly allowing the two halves to twist together. Smooth out any bumps by running your fingers up and down the cord and tie a knot to secure. You will now have a twisted cord approximately 92cm (36¼in) long.

FINISHING

Using mattress stitch, sew together the front and back of the bag by working down one side, across the bottom and up the other side.

Thread the twisted cords through the eyelets, starting and finishing at the centre front. Sew the two pompoms made out of yarn B to the twisted cord that is made out of yarn B and then the pompoms made out of yarn C to the twisted cord made out of yarn C. Position and attach the front and back of the magnetic snap to the knitted hems.

Make fabric lining as follows: Using the knitted bag as a template, cut two pieces of lining fabric slightly larger than the knitted pieces plus 1cm (⅜in) at the sides and the bottom for the seam allowance. Sew the two pieces together by working down one side, across the bottom and up the other side. Now, turn the

knitted bag inside out and with the lining fabric also inside out, sew the bottom two corners of the lining to the bottom two corners of the knitted bag. Fold the lining back over the bag and it will now look as if the whole bag has been turned inside out.

Place the wadding in between the knitted bag and the lining fabric and then slip stitch the hems at the top of the bag into place, at the same time securing and covering the top edges of the lining. Turn the bag right side out.

Sew handle into place inside the bag at the top of the side seams.

Sky

Big yarn, big needles! Why bother trying to squeeze all your essentials into a small bag? This oversized carry-all is a must for those who refuse to travel lightly. This is a very simple project, which you'll have knitted in no time at all.

SIZE
50cm × 30cm (20in × 12in)

MATERIALS
20mm (US 36) needles
6mm (US 10) needles

Yarn
Rowan Biggy Print
100g (3½oz) balls
   248 Splash (A)   4

Rowan Cotton Rope
50g (1¾oz) balls
   064 Calypso (B)   3

2 pieces, each measuring
57cm × 50cm (23in × 20in) lining
and wadding fabric (approximately)
Magnetic snap (Prym 416480)

TENSION (GAUGE)
5½ sts and 7 rows to 10cm (4in)
using 20mm (US 36) needles
measured over stocking
(stockinette) stitch.

ABBREVIATIONS
beg	beginning
k	knit
k2tog	knit two stitches together
p	purl
rem	remaining
RS	right side
sl	slip
st st	stocking (stockinette) stitch
sts	stitches
WS	wrong side

TECHNIQUES
Sewing up, see page 124
Blocking and pressing, see page 122

KNIT
Sides (make 2)
Using yarn A and 20mm (US 36) needles, cast on 25 sts.
ROW 1 (RS): **Knit.**
ROW 2 (WS): **Purl.**
Repeat last 2 rows once more ending with a WS row.
ROW 5: **K2tog, knit to last 2sts, k2tog. (23 sts)**
ROW 6: **Purl.**
ROW 7: **Knit.**
ROW 8: **Purl.**
ROW 9: **Knit.**
ROW 10: **Purl.**
ROW 11: **K2tog, knit to last 2sts, k2tog. (21 sts)**

Repeat rows 6–11 until 17sts remain, ending with a RS row.
ROW 18 (WS): **Knit.** (This creates garter-stitch ridge for turn over at top of bag.)
ROW 19: **Knit.**
ROW 20: **Purl.**
Repeat last 2 rows once more ending with a WS row.
Cast (bind) off.

Handles (make 2)
Using yarn B and 6mm (US 10) needles, cast on 9 sts.
ROW 1: **Knit.**
ROW 2: **K1, p7, k1.**
Repeat last 2 rows until work measures 130cm (51¾in), ending with a WS row.
Cast (bind) off.

sky's the limit

Soft, chunky yarn makes up the majority of this practical, yet highly stylish bag – while the tighter knitted handles add strength to allow for all those belongings.

FINISHING

Using mattress stitch, sew together the front and back of the bag by working down one side, across the bottom and up the other side.

Make fabric lining as follows: Using the knitted bag as a template, cut two pieces of lining fabric slightly larger than the knitted pieces plus 1cm (⅜in) at the sides and the bottom for the seam allowance. Sew the two pieces together by working down one side, across the bottom and up the other side. Now, turn the knitted bag inside out and with the lining fabric also inside out, sew the bottom two corners of the lining to the bottom two corners of the knitted bag. Fold the lining back over the bag and it will now look as if the whole bag has been turned inside out. Position and attach the front and back of the magnetic snap to the two pieces of lining fabric. Place the wadding in between the knitted bag and the lining fabric and then slip stitch the hems at the top of the bag into place, at the same time securing and covering the top edges of the lining. Turn the bag right side out.

Using the photograph as a guide, sew handles to the outside of the bag, positioning each handle 8cm (3¼in) in from each side seam.

Evening

After Eight

Accentuated with beadwork, this minted satchel is a must-have for any sophisticated occasion. With silver seed bead accents along the edge and strap, it's wonderfully versatile and works well with an array of stylish evening classics.

SIZE
25cm × 12cm (10in × 4¾in)

MATERIALS
4.5mm (US 7) needles

Yarn
Rowan Calmer
50g (1¾oz) balls
   474 Khaki   1

Approx. 370 Rowan Beads 01008 (Clear)
2 pieces, each measuring 35cm × 30cm (14in × 12in) lining and wadding fabric (approximately)
One small press stud

TENSION (GAUGE)
22 sts and 29 rows to 10cm (4in) using 4.5mm (US 7) needles measured over stocking (stockinette) stitch.

ABBREVIATIONS
beg   beginning
k   knit
p   purl
PB   place bead: yarn forward, slip bead to front of work, sl1 st purlwise, take yarn to back of work. Bead will now be sitting in front of slipped stitch.

rem remaining
RS   right side
sl   slip
st st stocking (stockinette) stitch
sts   stitches
WS   wrong side

TECHNIQUES
Sewing up, see page 124
Blocking and pressing, see page 122
Knitting with beads, see page 118

KNIT
Sides (make 2)
Using 4.5mm (US 7) needles, cast on 55 sts.
NOTE: Thread beads onto yarn before cast on.
ROW 1 (WS): Purl.
ROW 2 (RS): K1 (PB, k1) to end.
ROW 3: Purl.
ROW 4: K2 (PB, k1) to last 3 sts, PB, k2.
ROW 5: Purl.
ROW 6: K1 (PB, k1) to end.
ROW 7: Purl.
ROW 8: K1, PB, knit to last 2sts, PB, k1.
Repeat last 2 rows until work measures 12cm (4¾in) from cast on edge ending with a RS row.
NEXT ROW: Knit. (This creates garter-stitch for turn over at top of bag.)

NEXT ROW: Knit.
NEXT ROW: Purl.
Repeat last 2 rows once more ending with a WS row.
Cast (bind) off.

Handle
Thread approx. 150 beads onto a length of the yarn.

FINISHING
Using mattress stitch, sew together the front and back of the bag by working down one side, across the bottom and up the other side.

   Make fabric lining as follows: Using the knitted bag as a template, cut two pieces of lining fabric slightly larger than the

knitted pieces plus 1cm (⅜in) at the sides and the bottom for the seam allowance. Sew the two pieces together by working down one side, across the bottom and up the other side. Now, turn the knitted bag inside out and with the lining fabric also inside out, sew the bottom two corners of the lining to the bottom two corners of the knitted bag. Fold the lining back over the bag and it will now look as if the whole bag has been turned inside out.

Place the wadding in between the knitted bag and the lining fabric and then slip stitch the hems at the top of the bag into place, at the same time securing and covering the top edges of the lining. Turn the bag right side out.

Using the photograph as a guide, attach the handle by sewing neatly into place inside the side seams at the top of the bag.

Sew the press stud neatly and securely into place inside the top of the bag.

night sparkles

If you're interested in creating something unique and original, try beading the entire bag – you're guaranteed to make a bold statement!

Treasure

You can rest assured that this bag will stand out of the crowd. Simple lacework combined with some basic shaping creates this wonderfully shaped style. Add a touch of glam to your evening with this little number.

SIZE
27cm at widest point × 20cm (10¾in × 8in)

MATERIALS
4mm (US 6) needles

Yarn
Rowan 4ply Soft
50g (1¾oz) balls
    378 Daydream (A)   1
    (use double throughout)

Rowan Lurex Shimmer
25g (1oz) balls
    336 Gleam (B)   4
    (use double throughout)

2 pieces of lining and 4 pieces of wadding fabric, each measuring 57cm × 50cm (23in × 20in) (approximately)

TENSION (GAUGE)
22 sts and 30 rows to 10cm (4in) using 4mm (US 6) needles measured over stocking (stockinette) stitch.

ABBREVIATIONS
beg beginning
k   knit
p   purl
psso pass slipped stitch over
rem remaining
RS right side
sl slip
st st stocking (stockinette) stitch

sts stitches
WS wrong side
yf yarn forward

TECHNIQUES
Sewing up, see page 124
Blocking and pressing, see page 122

KNIT
Sides (make 2)
Using yarn B and 4mm (US 6) needles, cast on 61 sts.
Change to yarn A.
ROW 1: **Knit.**
ROW 2: **Purl.**
ROW 3: **Knit.**
Repeat last 2 rows three more times ending with a RS row.
Change to yarn B.
ROW 10: **Purl.**
ROW 11: **K1 (yf, sl1, k1, psso, k1, k2tog, yf, k1) to end.**
ROW 12: **Purl.**
ROW 13: **K2 (yf, sl1, k2tog, psso, yf, k3) to last 5 sts, yf, sl1, k2tog, psso, yf, k2.**
ROW 14: **Purl.**
Rows 11–14 form the pattern. Repeat these four rows until work measures 20cm (8in) ending with a RS row.

NEXT ROW: **Knit. (Dec 2 sts evenly across this row.) (59 sts)**
NEXT ROW: **K2, sl1, k1, psso (k3, sl1, k1, psso) to last 5 sts, k2, sl1, k1, psso, k1. (47 sts)**
NEXT ROW: **Purl.**
NEXT ROW: **K2, sl1, k1,**

psso (k2, sl1, k1, psso) to last 3 sts, k3. (36 sts)
NEXT ROW: **Purl.**
NEXT ROW: **K2, sl1, k1, psso (k1, sl1, k1, psso) to last 2 sts, k2. (25 sts)**
NEXT ROW: **Purl.**
NEXT ROW: **K1 (sl1, k1, psso) to end. (13 sts)**

NEXT ROW: **Purl.**

NEXT ROW: **K1 (sl1, k1, psso) to end. (7 sts)**

DO NOT cast (bind) off. Thread yarn through remaining stitches and pull together.

Fasten off.

Handle – twisted cord

Make a twisted cord using yarn A as follows:

Cut 4 lengths of yarn A approx. 188cm (74in) long. Take the four lengths of yarn and secure at each end with knots. Ask someone to help you and give her/him one end of the yarn while you hold the other. With the yarn outstretched, each end needs to be twisted in opposite directions until it shows signs of twisting back on itself. Bring the two ends of the cord together and hold tightly allowing the two halves to twist together. Smooth out any bumps by running your fingers up and down the cord and tie a knot to secure. You will now have a twisted cord approximately 75cm (29¼in) long.

FINISHING

Using mattress stitch, sew together the front and back of the bag by working down one side, around the bottom and up the other side.

Thread the twisted cord in and out of the lace about 2cm (1in) down from start of lace pattern.

Make fabric lining as follows: Using the knitted bag as a template, cut four pieces of lining fabric slightly larger than the knitted pieces plus 1cm (⅜in) at the sides and the bottom for the seam allowance. Sew a 1cm (⅜in) hem across the top edges of both pieces to neaten them up as they will be seen. Sew two of the pieces together by working down one side, across the bottom and up the other side. Now do the same with the other two pieces of fabric. You will now have two separate bag linings. Leave one inside out (so that the rough edges are showing) and turn the other one the right way out (so that the rough edges are on the inside). Put the inside out lining inside the other one. Turn the knitted bag inside out and sew the bottom two corners of the lining to the bottom two corners of the knitted bag. Fold the lining back over the bag and it will now look as if the whole bag has been turned inside out. Place the wadding in between the two layers of lining fabric and then slip stitch the lining into place around the top of the bag. Turn the bag right side out.

Gem

Toast the town! A delicate Fair Isle pattern worked in a glittering Lurex yarn adds instant verve to this free-spirited design enhanced with a garter-stitched trim at the top. A luxurious band of mohair lends a wispy aura of sophistication. Boasting intricate detail and soothing tones, this little gem is worth the effort!

SIZE
20cm × 21cm (8in × 8¼in)

MATERIALS
3.25mm (US 3) needles

Yarn
Rowan 4ply Soft
50g (1¾oz) balls
   387 Rain Cloud (A)   2

Rowan Kid Silk Night
25g (1oz) balls
   608 Moonlight (B)   1

Rowan Lurex Shimmer
25g (1oz) balls
   333 Pewter (C)   1

2 pieces, each measuring
35cm × 36cm (14in × 14in) lining
and wadding fabric (approximately)

TENSION (GAUGE)
28 sts and 36 rows to 10cm (4in)
using 3.25mm (US 3) needles
measured over stocking
(stockinette) stitch.

ABBREVIATIONS
beg beginning
k   knit
p   purl
rem remaining
RS   right side
sl   slip
st st stocking (stockinette) stitch

sts stitches
WS wrong side

TECHNIQUES
Sewing up, see page 124
Blocking and pressing, see page
122
Fair Isle, see page 117

KNIT
Front
Using yarn A and 3.25mm (US 3)
needles, cast on 57 sts.
Work rows 1–8 from chart over
page using the Fair Isle technique
as described on page 117.
Change to yarn B.
ROW 9: **Knit.**
ROW 10: **Knit.**
Repeat rows 1–10 seven more
times ending with a WS row.
Change to yarn A.
NEXT ROW: **Knit.**
Repeat this row six more
times ending with a WS
row.
Change to yarn B.
NEXT ROW: **Knit.**
Repeat this row six more
times ending with a WS row.
Change to yarn C.
NEXT ROW: **Knit.**
Repeat this row once more
ending with a WS row.
Change to yarn A.
ROW 1: **Knit.**
ROW 2: **Purl.**

Repeat last 2 rows two more times
ending with a WS row.
Cast (bind) off.

Back
Using yarn A and 3.25mm (US 3)
needles, cast on 57 sts.
ROW 1: **Knit.**
ROW 2: **Purl.**
Repeat last 2 rows
three more times
ending with a
WS row.
Change to
yarn B.
ROW 9:
Knit.

ROW 10: **Knit.**
Repeat rows 1–10 seven more
times ending with a WS row.
Change to yarn A.
NEXT ROW: **Knit.**
Repeat this row six more times
ending with a WS row.
Change to yarn B.
NEXT ROW: **Knit.**

CHART

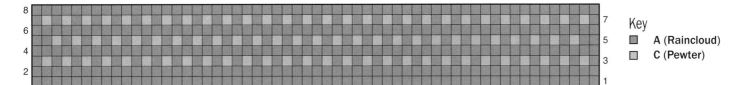

Key
- ☐ A (Raincloud)
- ☐ C (Pewter)

Repeat this row six more times ending with a WS row.
Change to yarn C.
NEXT ROW: **Knit.**
Repeat this row once more ending with a WS row.
Change to yarn A.
ROW 1: **Knit.**
ROW 2: **Purl.**
Repeat last 2 rows two more times ending with a WS row.
Cast (bind) off.

Handle – twisted cord

Make a twisted cord in yarn A as follows:
Cut 5 lengths of yarn A approx. 112cm (44in) long. Take the five lengths of yarn and secure at each end with knots. Ask someone to help you and give her/him one end of the yarn while you hold the other. With the yarn outstretched, each end needs to be twisted in opposite directions until it shows signs of twisting back on itself. Now bring the two ends of the cord together and hold tightly allowing the two halves to twist together. Smooth out any bumps by running your fingers up and down the cord and tie a knot to secure. You will now have a twisted cord approximately 45cm (17¾in) long. Tie a knot approx. 5cm (2in) in from each end, allowing the 5cm (2in) to unravel creating the 'tassels'. Sew each knot to the outside of the bag at the top of each side seam.

FINISHING

Using mattress stitch, sew together the front and back of the bag by working down one side, across the bottom and up the other side.

Make fabric lining as follows: Using the knitted bag as a template, cut two pieces of lining fabric slightly larger than the knitted pieces plus 1cm (⅜in) at the sides and the bottom for the seam allowance. Sew the two pieces together by working down one side, across the bottom and up the other side. Now, turn the knitted bag inside out and with the lining fabric also inside out, sew the bottom two corners of the lining to the bottom two corners of the knitted bag. Fold the lining back over the bag and it will now look as if the whole bag has been turned inside out.

Place the wadding in between the knitted bag and the lining fabric and then slip stitch the hems at the top of the bag into place, at the same time securing and covering the top edges of the lining. Turn the bag right side out.

Dash

If you're a girl on the go, it's always good to have a bag that holds everything! Metallic stripes and a variety of textures lend plenty of glamour and take this stunner from day to night without missing a beat.

SIZE
65cm at widest point × 37cm
(25¾in × 14½in)

MATERIALS
8mm (US 11) needles
10mm (US 15) needles

Yarn
Rowan Holiday
50g (1¾oz) balls
   035 Clover (A)   5

Rowan Glimmer Print
50g (1¾oz) balls
   002 Baroque (B)   5

Magnetic snap (Prym 416 480)
2 pieces, each measuring
106cm × 46cm (42in × 23in)
lining and wadding fabric
(approximately)

TENSION (GAUGE)
10 sts and 14 rows to 10cm (4in)
using using 8mm (US 11) needles
measured over stocking
(stockinette) stitch.

ABBREVIATIONS
beg	beginning
k	knit
k2tog	knit two stitches together
m1	make one stitch
p	purl
rem	remaining
RS	right side
sl	slip
st st	stocking (stockinette) stitch
sts	stitches
WS	wrong side

TECHNIQUES
Sewing up, see page 124
Blocking and pressing, see page
122

KNIT
Sides (make 2)
Using yarn A and 8mm (US 11)
needles, cast on 55 sts.
ROW 1 (RS): **Knit.**
ROW 2 (WS): **Purl.**
ROW 3: **Knit.**
Repeat last 2 rows twice more
ending with a RS row.
ROW 8: **Knit.** (This creates
garter-stitch ridge for turn over at
top of bag.)
Change to yarn B.
ROW 9: **Knit.**
ROW 10: **Purl.**
Repeat last 2 rows once more,
ending with a WS row.
Change to yarn A.
ROW 13: **Knit.**
ROW 14: **Knit.**
Change to yarn B.
ROW 15: **Knit.**
ROW 16: **Purl.**
Repeat last 2 rows twice more,
ending with a WS row.
Place markers on the 5th, 14th,
23rd, 32nd, 41st and 50th stitches.

You should have six marked
stitches in total.
ROW 21 (INC ROW): **K4, m1, k marked
st, m1 (k8, m1, k marked st, m1) to
last 5 sts, k5. (67 sts)**
Change to yarn A.
ROW 22: **Purl.**
ROW 23: **Knit.**
Repeat last 2 rows twice more,
ending with a WS row.
ROW 28: **Purl.**
ROW 29 (INC ROW): **K5, m1, k marked
st, m1 (k10, m1, k marked st, m1)
to last 6 sts, k6. (79 sts)**
ROW 30: **Purl.**
Change to yarn B.
ROW 31: **Knit.**
Repeat last row five more times,
ending with a WS row.
ROW 37 (INC ROW): **K6, m1, k marked
st, m1 (k12, m1, k marked st, m1)
to last 7 sts, k7. (91sts)**
ROW 38: **Knit.**
Change to yarn A.
Repeat last row eight more times,
ending with a WS row.
Change to yarn B.
ROW 43 (DEC ROW): **K5, k2tog, k
marked st, k2tog (k10, k2tog, k
marked st, k2tog) to last 6 sts, K6.
(79 sts)**
ROW 44: **Knit.**
Repeat last row four more times,
ending with a WS row.
Change to yarn A.
ROW 49 (DEC ROW): **K4, k2tog, k
marked st, k2tog (k8, k2tog, k
marked st, k2tog) to last 5, k5.
(67 sts)**

ROW 50: **Knit.**
Repeat last row four more times,
ending with a WS row.
Change to yarn B.
ROW 55 (DEC ROW): **K3, k2tog, k
marked st, k2tog (k6, k2tog, k
marked st, k2tog) to last 4 sts, k4.
(55 sts)**
ROW 56: **Knit.**
Repeat last row twice more, ending
with a WS row.
ROW 59 (DEC ROW): **K2, k2tog, k
marked st, k2tog (k4, k2tog, k
marked st, k2tog) to last 3 sts, k3.
(43 sts)**
ROW 60: **Knit.**
Repeat last row twice more ending
with a WS row.
ROW 61 (DEC ROW): **K1, k2tog, k
marked st, k2tog (k2, k2tog, k
marked st, k2tog) to last 2 sts, k2.
(31 sts)**
ROW 62: **Knit.**
Cast (bind) off.

Handle
Using yarn A and 10mm (US 15)
needles, cast on 9 sts.
ROW 1: **Knit.**
Repeat last row until work
measures 100cm (39¼in) from
cast on edge, ending with a WS
row.
Cast (bind) off.

FINISHING

Using mattress stitch, sew together the front and back of the bag by working down one side, across the bottom and up the other side.

Position and attach the front and back of the magnetic snap to the knitted hems.

Make fabric lining as follows: Using the knitted bag as a template, cut two pieces of lining fabric slightly larger than the knitted pieces plus 1cm (⅜in) at the sides and the bottom for the seam allowance. Sew the two pieces together by working down one side, across the bottom and up the other side. Now, turn the knitted bag inside out and with the lining fabric also inside out, sew the bottom two corners of the lining to the bottom two corners of the knitted bag. Fold the lining back over the bag and it will now look as if the whole bag has been turned inside out.

Place the wadding in between the knitted bag and the lining fabric and then slip stitch the hems at the top of the bag into place, at the same time securing and covering the top edges of the lining. Turn the bag right side out.

Sew handle into place inside the bag at the top of the side seams.

bags of style

This bag is so chic and now, it makes an ideal gift. Stitch one for your favourite gal pal in an assortment of colours. Big needles and chunky yarn make it super-quick to knit!

Soirée

A striking intarsia pattern adorns the front of this clutch bag while pretty chain stitch detailing around the motifs provides extra definition to the design. Embellished with a scattering of silver beads, this bold bag makes a winning statement.

SIZE
29cm × 19cm (11½in × 7½in)

MATERIALS
4mm (US 6) needles

Yarn
Rowan Wool cotton
50g (1¾oz) balls
   955 Shipshape (A)   2

Rowan Lurex Shimmer
25g (1oz) balls
   339 Midnight (B)   1
   (use double throughout)
   333 Pewter (C)   1
   (use double throughout)

Rowan 4ply Cotton
50g (1¾oz) balls
   121 Ripple (D)   1
   (use double throughout)

Approx. 9 Rowan Beads 01008
(Clear)
2 pieces, each measuring
44cm × 34cm (18in × 13in) lining
and wadding fabric (approximately)

TENSION (GAUGE)
22 sts and 32 rows to 10cm (4in)
using 4mm (US 6) needles
measured over stocking
(stockinette) stitch.

ABBREVIATIONS
beg   beginning
k   knit
p   purl
rem   remaining
RS   right side
sl   slip
st st   stocking (stockinette) stitch
sts   stitches
WS   wrong side

TECHNIQUES
Sewing up, see page 124
Blocking and pressing, see page 122
Intarsia, see page 116

KNIT
Front
Using yarn A and 4mm (US 6)
needles, cast on 65 sts.
ROW 1: **Knit.**
ROW 2: **Purl.**
Repeat last 2 rows two more times,
ending with a WS row.
Now work rows 1–30 from the
chart, on the page overleaf, ending
with a WS row using the intarsia
technique as described on page
116.
ROW 37: **Knit.**
ROW 38: **Purl.**
Repeat last 2 rows until work
measures 16cm (6¼in) from cast

on edge ending with a WS row.
NEXT ROW: **Knit 20, cast (bind) off
centre 25 sts, knit to end.**
NEXT ROW: **Purl 20, turn, cast on
centre 25 sts, turn, purl to end.**
NEXT ROW: **Knit.**
NEXT ROW: **Purl.**
Repeat last 2 rows three more
times ending with a WS row.
NEXT ROW: **Knit.**
NEXT ROW: **Knit. (This creates the
garter-stitch ridge for the turn over
at the top.)**
NEXT ROW: **Knit.**
NEXT ROW: **Purl.**
Repeat last 2 rows three more
times ending with a WS row.

NEXT ROW: **Knit.**
NEXT ROW: **Purl 20, cast (bind) off
centre 25 sts, purl to end.**
NEXT ROW: **Knit 20, turn, cast on
centre 25 sts, turn, knit to end.**
NEXT ROW: **Purl.**
NEXT ROW: **Knit.**
NEXT ROW: **Purl.**
Repeat last 2 rows once more
ending with a WS row.
Cast (bind) off.

BACK
Using yarn A and 4mm (US 6)
needles, cast on 65 sts.
ROW 1: **Knit.**

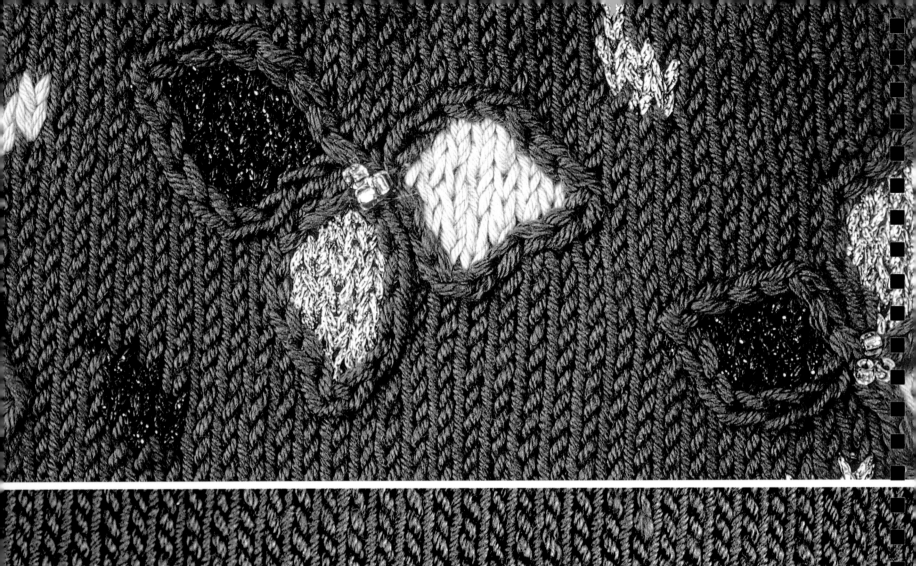

CHART

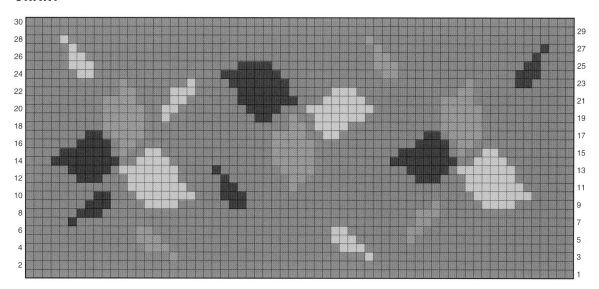

Key
- ▢ A (Shipshape)
- ▨ B (Midnight)
- ▪ C (Pewter)
- ▫ D (Ripple)

ROW 2: **Purl.**
Repeat last 2 rows until work measures 16cm (6¼in) from cast on edge ending with a WS row.
NEXT ROW: **Knit 20, cast (bind) off centre 25 sts, knit to end.**
NEXT ROW: **Purl 20, turn, cast on centre 25 sts, turn, purl to end.**
NEXT ROW: **Knit.**
NEXT ROW: **Purl.**
Repeat last 2 rows three more times ending with a WS row.
NEXT ROW: **Knit.**
NEXT ROW: **Knit. (This creates the garter-stitch ridge for the turn over at the top.)**
NEXT ROW: **Knit.**
NEXT ROW: **Purl.**
Repeat last 2 rows three more times ending with a WS row.
NEXT ROW: **Knit.**
NEXT ROW: **Purl 20, cast (bind) off centre 25 sts, purl to end.**
NEXT ROW: **Knit 20, turn, cast on centre 25 sts, turn, knit to end.**
NEXT ROW: **Purl.**
NEXT ROW: **Knit.**
NEXT ROW: **Purl.**
Repeat last 2 rows once more ending with a WS row.
Cast (bind) off.

FINISHING

Using mattress stitch, sew together the front and back of the bag by working down one side, across the bottom and up the other side.

Using the photograph as a guide and yarn A, chain stitch around each of the three leaves making up each motif. Sew a cluster of three beads into the centre of each motif.

Make fabric lining as follows:
NOTE: This bag is being lined with fabric from the handle down. The handle has been knitted as a double layer and this will act as the lining for this area.

Using the knitted bag as a template, cut two pieces of lining fabric slightly larger than the knitted pieces plus 1cm (⅜in) at the sides and the bottom for the seam allowance. Sew the two pieces together by working down one side, across the bottom and up the other side. Now, turn the knitted bag inside out and with the lining fabric also inside out, sew the bottom two corners of the lining to the bottom two corners of the knitted bag. Fold the lining back over the bag and it will now look as if the whole bag has been turned inside out.

Place the wadding in between the knitted bag and the lining fabric. Also, pad the handle with wadding and then turn over the knitted hems and slip stitch into place, at the same time securing and covering the top edges of the lining. Turn the bag right side out.

Cherry Drop

When you're ready to paint the town red, this pouch is the perfect place to keep your belongings. Featuring a simple all-over rib pattern and a sparkly Lurex I-cord to wrap around your wrist, it's effortlessly chic and incredibly easy to make.

SIZE
18cm at widest point × 19cm
(7in × 7½in)

MATERIALS
5mm (US 8) needles
4mm (US 6) double pointed
needles

Yarn
Rowan Calmer
50g (1¾oz) balls
476 Coral (A)   1

Rowan Lurex Shimmer
25g (1oz) balls
331 Claret (B)   1
(used double throughout)

2 pieces, each measuring
33cm × 34cm (13in × 13in) lining
and wadding fabric (approximately)

TENSION (GAUGE)
21 sts and 30 rows to 10cm (4in)
using 5mm (US 8) needles
measured over stocking
(stockinette) stitch.

ABBREVIATIONS
beg	beginning
k	knit
p	purl
psso	pass slipped stitch over
p2tog	purl two stitches together
rem	remaining
RS	right side

sl	slip
st st	stocking (stockinette) stitch
sts	stitches
WS	wrong side
yf	yarn forward

TECHNIQUES
Sewing up, see page 124
Blocking and pressing, see page 122

KNIT
Sides (make 2)
Using yarn B and 5mm (US 8)
needles, cast on 153 sts.
ROW 1: **K1, *k2 lift first of these 2 over second, rep from * to end.** (77 sts)
ROW 2: **(P2tog) to last st, p1.** (39 sts)
Change to yarn A.
ROW 3: **Knit.**
Repeat this row seven more times ending with a WS row.
ROW 11: **Knit.**
ROW 12: **Purl.**
ROW 13 (EYELET ROW): **K4 (yf, k2tog, k4) to last 5 sts, yf, k2tog, k3.**
ROW 14: **Purl.**
ROW 15: **Knit.**
ROW 16: **K1 (p1, k1) to end.**
Repeat last two rows twenty more times, ending with a WS row.
ROW 57: **K2, sl1, k1, psso (k3, sl1, k1, psso) to last 5 sts, k2, sl1, k1, psso, k1.** (31 sts)
ROW 58: **Purl.**

on the ropes
When making the knitted cord for the drawstring on this bag, the challenge is not to turn at the end of each row. Remember, you are always knitting, never purling.

ROW 59: **K2, sl1, k1, psso (k2, sl1, k1, psso)** to last 3 sts, **k3.** (24 sts)
ROW 60: **Purl.**
ROW 60: **Purl.**
ROW 61: **K2, sl1, k1, psso (k1, sl1, k1, psso)** to last 2 sts, **k2.** (17 sts)
ROW 62: **Purl.**
ROW 63: **K1 (sl1, k1, psso)** to end. (9 sts)
ROW 64: **Purl.**
ROW 65: **K1 (sl1, k1, psso)** to end. (5 sts)
DO NOT cast (bind) off. Thread yarn through remaining stitches and pull together.
Fasten off.

Drawstring cord

NOTE: The drawstring is made using a technique sometimes known as either a 'knitted cord' or an 'I-cord'. Once you have cast on your stitches, you knit one row. You would now usually turn your needles but to make the I-cord DO NOT TURN. Instead, slide the stitches to the other end of the double pointed needle ready to be knitted again. The yarn will now be at the left edge of the knitting and so to knit you must pull it tightly across the back of your work and then knit one row. You continue in this way, never turning and always sliding the work to the other end of the double pointed needle and the right side of the work will always be facing you.
Using the technique as described, make the drawstring cord as follows:
Using yarn B and 4mm (US 6) double pointed needles, cast on 4 sts.
ROW 1: **Knit.**
Repeat this row until work measures 60cm (23½in) from cast on edge.

DO NOT cast (bind) off. Thread yarn through remaining stitches and pull together.
Fasten off.

FINISHING

Using mattress stitch, sew together the front and back of the bag by working down one side, across the bottom and up the other side.

Make fabric lining as follows:
Using the knitted bag as a template, cut out two pieces of lining fabric slightly larger than the knitted pieces plus 1cm (⅜in) all the way round for the seam allowance. Sew a 1cm (⅜in) hem across the top edges of both pieces to neaten them up as they will be seen. Sew the two pieces together by working down one side, across the bottom and up the other side.

Now, turn the knitted bag inside out and with the lining fabric also inside out, sew the bottom two corners of the lining to the bottom two corners of the knitted bag. Keeping the knitted bag inside out, turn the fabric lining back over the bag. It will now look as if the whole bag has been turned inside out. Place the wadding in between the knitted bag and the lining fabric. Thread the I-cord through the eyelets and then slip stitch the lining into place around the top of the bag. Turn the bag right side out.

Vintage

Flirty and feminine, this lacy cherry-red number makes a wickedly subtle and understated accompaniment to any evening dress. Open it up to reveal a wonderful lining and space enough for all your necessities – why not let this bag add a touch of drama to your collection?

SIZE
21cm × 25cm (8¼in × 10in)

MATERIALS
3.25mm (US 3) needles

Yarn
Rowan Cotton Glace
50g (1¾oz) balls
   445 Blood Orange   2

Acrylic Handles (Prym 615 105)
4 pieces of lining fabric and 2
pieces of wadding, each measuring
36cm × 40cm (14in × 16in)
(approximately)

TENSION (GAUGE)
21 sts and 29 rows to 10cm (4in)
using 3.25mm (US 3) needles
measured over pattern.

ABBREVIATIONS
beg   beginning
k   knit
p   purl
rem   remaining
RS   right side
sl   slip
st st   stocking (stockinette) stitch
sts   stitches
WS   wrong side

TECHNIQUES
Sewing up, see page 124
Blocking and pressing, see page
122

KNIT
Sides (make 2)
Using 3.25mm (US 3) needles, cast
on 43 sts.
ROW 1: **K1 (yf, sl1, k1, psso, k1,
k2tog, yf, k1) to end.**
ROW 2: **Purl.**
ROW 3: **K2 (yf, sl1, k2tog, psso, yf,
k3) to last 5 sts, yf, sl1, k2tog, psso,
yf, k2.**
ROW 4: **Purl.**
These four rows form the pattern.
Repeat these four rows until work
measures 25cm (10in) from cast
on edge ending with a WS row.
NEXT ROW: **Knit.**
NEXT ROW: **Knit. (This creates
garter-stitch ridge for turn over at
top of bag.)**
NEXT ROW: **Knit.**
NEXT ROW: **Purl.**
Repeat last 2 rows once more
ending with a WS row.
Cast (bind) off.

red alert

You don't have to stick with the handles we've chosen – you
could try knitting your own handles or select a different shade of
acrylic handle. It's up to you!

FINISHING

Using mattress stitch, sew together the front and back of the bag by working down one side, across the bottom and up the other side.

Make fabric lining as follows: Using the knitted bag as a template, cut four pieces of lining fabric slightly larger than the knitted pieces plus 1cm (⅜in) at the sides and the bottom for the seam allowance. Sew two of the pieces together by working down one side, across the bottom and up the other side. Now do the same with the other two pieces of fabric. You will now have two separate bag linings. Leave one inside out (so that the rough edges are showing) and turn the other one the right way out (so that the rough edges are on the inside). Now, put the inside out lining inside the other one. Next, turn the knitted bag inside out and sew the bottom two corners of the lining to the bottom two corners of the knitted bag. Fold the lining back over the bag and it will now look as if the whole bag has been turned inside out.

Place the wadding in between the two layers of lining fabric and then slip stitch the hems at the top of the bag into place, at the same time securing and covering the top edges of the lining. Turn the bag right side out.

Using the photograph as a guide, attach the handles by sewing neatly into place inside the top of the bag.

Caramel

Be as impulsive with your accessories as you are with your clothes – this makes a timeless and elegant companion to any evening ensemble. A scatter of gold sequins adds a sense of luxury and style, while catching the light as you dance across the floor.

SIZE
24cm × 21cm (9¾in × 8¼in)

MATERIALS
3.25mm (US 3) needles

Yarn
Rowan 4ply Soft
50g (1¾oz) balls
389 Expresso (A)	1
386 Irish Cream (B)	1

Approx. 84 Gold sequins – small
Approx. 28 Gold sequins – large
2 pieces, each measuring
39cm × 37cm (15in × 14in) lining
and wadding fabric (approximately)
Magnetic snap (Prym 416480)

TENSION (GAUGE)
28 sts and 36 rows to 10cm (4in)
using 3.25mm (US 3) needles
measured over stocking
(stockinette) stitch.

ABBREVIATIONS
beg beginning
k knit
p purl
PLS Place Larger Sequin: yarn forward, slip sequin to front of work, sl1 st purlwise, take yarn to back of work. Sequin will now be sitting in front of the slipped stitch.
PSS Place Smaller Sequin: yarn forward, slip sequin to front of work, sl1 st purlwise, take yarn to back of work. Sequin will now be sitting in front of the slipped stitch.
rem remaining
RS right side
sl slip
st st stocking (stockinette) stitch
sts stitches
WS wrong side

TECHNIQUES
Sewing up, see page 124
Blocking and pressing, see page 122
Knitting with sequins, see page 120

KNIT
Sides (make 2)
Using yarn A and 3.25mm (US 3) needles, cast on 59 sts.
ROW 1: **Knit.**
ROW 2: **Purl.**
Repeat last 2 rows three more times ending with a WS row.
ROW 9: **Knit.**
ROW 10: **Knit. (This creates garter-stitch ridge.)**
Change to yarn B.
ROW 11: **Knit.**
ROW 12: **Purl.**
ROW 13: **(K3, PSS) to last 3 sts, k3.**
ROW 14: **Purl.**
ROW 15: **Knit.**
ROW 16: **Purl.**
ROW 17: **K5 (PSS, k3) to last 6 sts, PSS, k5.**
ROW 18: **Purl.**
ROW 19: **Knit.**
ROW 20: **Purl.**
ROW 21: **(K3, PSS) to last 3 sts, k3.**
ROW 22: **Purl.**
ROW 23: **(K3, PLS) to last 3 sts, k3.**
ROW 24: **Purl.**
ROW 25: **Knit.**
ROW 26: **Purl.**
Change to yarn A.
ROW 27: **Knit.**
ROW 28: **Purl.**
Repeat last 2 rows until work measures 22cm (8½in) from garter-stitch ridge, ending with a WS row.
Cast (bind) off.

Handle
Using yarn A and 3.25mm (US 3) needles, cast on 5 sts.
ROW 1: **Knit.**
ROW 2: **K1, p3, k1.**

sparkles and light

Before you start knitting this bag, you must thread the sequins onto the yarn. Follow the instructions for knitting with sequins as outlined on page 120.

Repeat last 2 rows until work measures 32cm (12¾in) from cast on edge ending with a **WS** row. Cast (bind) off.

FINISHING

Using mattress stitch, sew together the front and back of the bag by working down one side, across the bottom and up the other side.

Make fabric lining as follows: Using the knitted bag as a template, cut two pieces of lining fabric slightly larger than the knitted pieces plus 1cm (¾in) at the sides and the bottom for the seam allowance. Sew the two pieces together by working down one side, across the bottom and up the other side. Now, turn the knitted bag inside out and with the lining fabric also inside out, sew the bottom two corners of the lining to the bottom two corners of the knitted bag. Fold the lining back over the bag and it will now look as if the whole bag has been turned inside out. Position and attach the front and back of the magnetic snap to the two pieces of lining fabric. Place the wadding in between the knitted bag and the lining fabric and then slip stitch the hems at the top of the bag into place, at the same time securing and covering the top edges of the lining. Turn the bag right side out. Sew handle into place inside the bag at the top of the side seams.

Techniques

INTARSIA KNITTING

Intarsia knitting produces a single thickness fabric that uses different balls of yarn for different areas of colour. There should be very little, if any, carrying across of yarns at the back of the work.

There are several ways to help keep the separate colours of yarn organized while you are working. My preferred method is to use yarn bobbins. Small amounts of yarn can be wound onto bobbins, which should then be kept close to the back of the work while knitting, and only unwound when more yarn is needed.

The intarsia patterns in this book are given in the form of a chart. It is advisable to make a colour copy of the chart and to enlarge it if you prefer. This copy can be used as a worksheet on which rows can be marked off as they are worked and any notes can be made.

Joining in a new colour

1 Insert the right needle into the next stitch. Place the end of the new pink yarn between the tips of the needles and across the purple yarn from left to right.

2 Take the new pink yarn under the purple yarn and knit the next stitch with it. Carefully move the tail of pink yarn off the right needle as the new stitch is formed.

Changing colours

To avoid gaps between stitches when changing colour, it is essential that the two yarns are crossed over at the back of the work.

1 On a knit row, insert the right needle into the next stitch. Place the old purple yarn over the new pink yarn. Pull the new pink yarn up and knit the stitch.

2 On a purl row, insert the right needle into the next stitch. Place the old pink yarn over the new purple yarn. Pull the new purple yarn up and purl the next stitch.

Sewing in ends

When an intarsia area is completed, there will be loose ends to darn in on the back of the work.

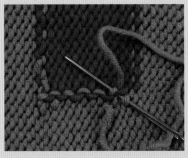 

1 Darn the ends around shapes by darning through the loops of the same colour in one direction first.

2 Then darn the end back on itself, stretching the work before cutting the end of the yarn.

FAIR ISLE KNITTING

Stranding is used when the yarn not in use is left at the back of the work until needed. The loops formed by stranding are called 'floats', and it is important to ensure that they are not pulled too tightly when working the next stitch as this will pull in your knitting. If the gap between the colours is more than four stitches, the weaving-in method (described right) is preferable as this prevents too long floats that stop the fabric having the right amount of elasticity. Many colour patterns will use both techniques and you will choose the one that is the most appropriate to a particular part of the design.

Stranding

1 On a knit row, hold the first colour in your right hand and the second colour in your left hand. Knit the required number of stitches as usual with the first colour, carrying the second colour loosely across the wrong side of the work.

2 To knit a stitch in the second colour, insert the right-hand needle into the next stitch, then draw a loop through from the yarn held in the left hand – carrying the yarn in the right hand loosely across the wrong side until required.

3 On a purl row, hold the yarns as for the knit rows. Purl the required number of stitches as usual with the first colour, carrying the second colour loosely across these stitches on the wrong side of the work.

4 To purl a stitch in the second colour, insert the right-hand needle into the next stitch then draw a loop through from the yarn held in the left hand, carrying the yarn in the right hand loosely across the wrong side until next required.

Weaving

Weaving in, or knitting in, the floats are caught in by the working yarn on every alternate stitch, or preferably on every third or fourth stitch. (Weaving in on every alternate stitch can distort the stitches and alter the tension.)

Insert the right-hand needle into the stitch. Lay the contrast yarn over the point of the right-hand needle then knit the stitch in the usual way, taking care not to knit in the contrast yarn. When you knit the next stitch, the contrast yarn will have been caught in. Use the same method to catch in the yarn on the purl rows.

1 On a knit row, hold the first colour in your right hand and the second colour in your left hand. Knit the required number of rows.

Fancy Yarns

Colour knitting offers a wonderful opportunity to incorporate fancy yarns into garments. Gold and silver Lurex yarns tend to look garish on their own, but can add subtle sparkle and a touch of glamour to knitwear when used in small quantities. Try working Lurex into a Fair Isle pattern to give a new touch to a traditional design. Mohair and angora yarns can work well too. Do experiment with combining different types of yarn; the results can be wonderful.

KNITTING WITH BEADS

There are many different types of beads available, but not all of them are suitable for hand knitting. When choosing beads it is important to check that the bead hole is big enough for the yarn to pass through. In addition, the weight and size of the beads also need to be considered. For example, large heavy beads on 4-ply knitting will look clumsy and cause the fabric to sag. It is also wise to check whether the beads you are using are washable, as some may not be.

When you have chosen your beads, you must thread them onto the yarn before you start to knit. There is a very easy way to do this.

Threading beads onto yarn

Place a length of sewing cotton beneath the yarn, then bring the two ends of the cotton together and thread both ends through a sewing needle. Thread the beads onto the needle, then push them down the sewing cotton and onto the knitting yarn. Remember that the first bead you thread onto the yarn will be the last one to be knitted in.

ADDING BEADS WITH A SLIP STITCH

This is my preferred method of adding beads to knitting, and it works on both wrong-side and right-side rows. The beads sit in front of a slipped stitch and hang down slightly from where they are knitted in. I have found that if the yarn is held quite firmly and the next stitch after the bead is knitted tightly, the bead sits very neatly and snugly against the knitting.

Adding beads on a right side row

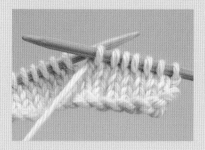

1 Work to where the bead is to be placed. Bring the yarn forward between the points of the needles.

2 Push a bead up the yarn to the front of the work, so that it rests in front of the right-hand needle.

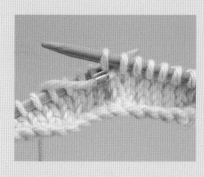

3 Slip the next stitch purlwise from the left-hand to the right-hand needle, leaving the bead in front of the slipped stitch.

4 Take the yarn between the needles to the back of the work and continue in pattern. The bead is now secured in position.

Adding beads on a wrong side row

When beads are placed on a wrong side row, the instructions are almost the same.

1 When a bead is to be added, take the yarn back between the needle points and push a bead up to the front of the work.

2 Slip the next stitch exactly as for adding beads on a right side row.

3 Bring the yarn forward and continue working. On the next row work the slip stitch firmly.

Adding beads to reverse stocking (stockinette) stitch

The principle is the same. Place the bead with the yarn at front of work. Slide a bead up so that it rests in front of the right-hand needle. Slip the next stitch purlwise and keeping yarn at front of work pull firmly so that bead sits in front of slipped stitch then purl the next stitch.

KNITTING WITH SEQUINS

Some sequins are plain in colour, but there are others that resemble mini-holograms, and these create quite spectacular multicoloured effects when held in the light. Sequins not only add extra colour and sparkle to a knitted fabric, but they also change the quality and feel of the knitting.

When choosing sequins, it is important to remember that the hole through the centre must be big enough for the yarn to pass through. The size of the sequin should also be considered, and chosen in relation to the weight of yarn used. And, as with beads, it is also best to check if the sequins are washable before buying them.

The method of adding sequins to knitting is identical to the way that beads are knitted in. However, care should be taken to hold the sequins flat to the fabric while knitting, ensuring that they are all lying the same way. And it is advisable only to place sequins while working on a right side row, as it is extremely difficult to do this on a wrong side row.

CABLES

Cables are the crossing of one set of stitches over another to create a twisted rope effect. Stitches can be crossed over at the front or the back of the work; this determines whether the cable twists to the left or to the right. Stitches held at the front of the work will twist the cable to the left, stitches held at the back of the work will twist the cable to the right. Cables are usually knitted in stocking (stockinette) stitch on a background of reverse stocking (stockinette) stitch, though a background of stocking (stockinette) stitch can also work well. Usually the number of stitches that are crossed is half of the amount stated in the abbreviation, ie: C8B means cross 4 stitches with 4 stitches. There are many different variations, so it is best to read the instructions carefully before starting to knit. This example shows how to work C8B.

C8B

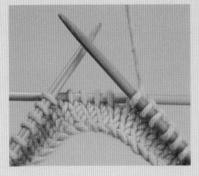

1 Slip the next 4 stitches onto the cable needle and hold at the back of the work.

2 Knit 4 stitches from the left-hand needle.

3 Then knit the 4 stitches that are on the cable needle.

4 Make sure that you pull the yarn firmly and knit the stitches tightly to avoid any gaps in the work.

ADDING EMBROIDERY TO KNITTING

Outlines, single dots, or fancy shapes and textures can be added to your fabric after knitting. It is advisable to finish your knitting and tidy up the loose ends before embroidering. A large, blunt darning needle should be used to avoid splitting the stitches. A yarn of the same or a slightly heavier weight as the main knitting that will easily cover the stitches is recommended.

I have used Swiss darning in various projects in this book. This is a method of duplicating knitted stitches on stocking (stockinette) stitch fabrics using a needle and a separate length of yarn. It is a quick and easy way of adding dashes of colour or outlines, and it can be worked horizontally or vertically.

BLOCKING AND PRESSING

The blocking and pressing of knitting is an essential part of the finishing process, and one that is often omitted by knitters. There are several reasons why blocking and pressing should be done. Firstly, it flattens the edges of the knitting, which makes it easier to pick up stitches or sew together panels. Secondly, it ensures that the panels are the correct size. And lastly, it finishes the knitted fabric, and in most cases changes the physical quality of the knitting, smoothing out stitches and making the fabric feel softer and more fluid.

Blocking is the pinning out of the knitted pieces, which should be done on a flat surface with the wrong side facing up. A tape measure should be used to ensure that the pieces are of the correct size. The temperature of the iron used for pressing is dependant on the fibre content of the yarn, as is the damp or dry pressing cloth, which must completely cover the panel that is going to be pressed. The general rule is as follows: natural fibres require a damp pressing cloth and a warm iron, and synthetic fibres and mixes require a dry pressing cloth and a cool iron. However, not all yarns conform to these rules and some have alternative requirements, so it is always advisable to read the pressing instructions that are printed on the ball band. If several different yarns have been used in one piece of knitting, it is better to play safe and follow the instructions for the most delicate yarn. If the heat of the iron is too hot, it could ruin the knitting permanently, resulting in a limp and lifeless piece of knitting – damage that is irreversible.

After pressing it is best to leave the knitting pinned out for at least half an hour to allow all of the heat and moisture to evaporate. Then, when the pins are removed, the knitting will be flat and ready for sewing up.

BAG CARE

Hand-washing

Your bag should be hand-washed to maintain its quality. Use plenty of lukewarm water and a detergent specially formulated for knitwear. The fabric should be gently squeezed and then rinsed in several changes of water. It is a good idea to get rid of excess water by gently spinning the bag in a washing-machine inside a secure wash-bag, such as a pillowcase, to avoid the fabric stretching. This will also protect any beads or buttons. Lay the bag out flat on a towel after washing, and gently ease back into shape. It should then be left alone until it is completely dry.

Dry-cleaning

You can have your bag dry-cleaned, but check that all of the yarns used can be dry-cleaned. Remember that if beads or buttons have been used, the dry-cleaners may refuse to clean it.

SEWING UP

After spending time knitting your bag, it is very important that the sewing together of the panels is done as neatly as possible. I would recommend that you use mattress stitch, because it is easy to learn, very precise and it creates an almost invisible seam. One big advantage of using this stitch over other methods of sewing up is that you work with the right sides of the knitting facing up towards you, which enables you to see exactly how the seam is progressing. Mattress stitch also allows you to accurately match stripes or patterns on the back and front panels of the bag.

A blunt sewing-up needle and a matching yarn should be used to sew together the panels. Lay the pieces of knitting out on a flat surface in the arrangement in which they are to be sewn together.

Mattress stitch seam (sewing stitches to stitches)

1 From the back of the work, insert the needle through the centre of the first stitch along one of the edges, leaving a long tail of yarn.

2 From the back of the work, insert the needle between the first and the second stitches along the opposite edge.

3 Continue in this way, zigzagging backwards and forwards from edge to edge, and pulling the stitches up to close the seam. Do not pull too hard or the seam will be too tight.

4 The mattress seam is invisible on the right side. Continue sewing the whole seam, then secure the ends by darning them in.

Mattress stitch seam (sewing rows to rows)

1 From the front, insert the needle between the first and second stitches on the first row. Take the needle under the next row and bring it through to the front again. Pull the yarn through, leaving a long end.

2 Insert the needle the same way into the other edge that is to be joined, but this time bring the needle out two rows above the point where it goes in.

3 Insert the needle into the first edge again, into the hole that the thread last came out of on that edge. Bring the needle out two rows above that point.

4 Repeat, zigzagging from edge to edge for 5cm (2in). Pull the thread up, holding the seam and long end of the yarn with the left hand.

YARN INFORMATION

Choosing the right yarn

If you want your knitted bag to look like the picture in the book, I would recommend that you use the yarns that I have specified for each design. A substitute yarn that differs in weight, shade, or fibre content will change the whole look, feel, and size of the finished bag.

Quantities of yarn and dye lots

At the beginning of each project the quantities of yarn are given for the bag. If different yarns are used, these quantities will alter. This is because the length of a ball of yarn depends on its weight and fibre content: an aran weight cotton will have a shorter length than an aran weight wool, and a 4-ply cotton will have a longer length than a double-knit cotton. The quantities of yarn can be re-calculated if desired. Buy all the yarn you need to complete the project at the same time, checking the ball bands to ensure that all the balls are from the same dye lot. The colour of a specific shade of yarn can vary quite a lot between dye lots and the change will show in the finished project.

Tension (Gauge) and selecting correct needle size

The needle sizes that I have recommended for each design have been chosen to create a firm tension (gauge). This is especially important if you are knitting accessories that are going to be handled, such as bags. If the knitting is too loose, the article will easily become misshapen, and will most likely drop, and grow in size. Using a slightly smaller needle than the usual recommended size for the yarn ensures that the knitted fabric retains its shape.

Tension (gauge) can differ quite dramatically between knitters. This is because of the way that the needles and the yarn are held. So if your tension (gauge) does not match that stated in the pattern, you should change your needle size following this simple rule:

- If your knitting is too loose, your tension (gauge) will read that you have fewer stitches and rows than the given tension (gauge), and you will need to change to a thinner needle to make the stitch size smaller.
- If your knitting is too tight, your tension (gauge) will read that you have more stitches and rows than the given tension (gauge), and you will need to change to a thicker needle to make the stitch size bigger.

Note that if the projects in this book are not knitted to the correct tension (gauge), yarn quantities will be affected.

YARN USED IN THIS BOOK

A selection of yarns from the Rowan Yarn collection have been used to knit all of the designs in this book. Below is a guide to the yarns used.

All Seasons Cotton
Aran-weight cotton and microfibre yarn
60% cotton/40% microfibre
Approximately 90m (98yds) per
    50g (1¾oz) ball

Biggy Print
Super chunky pure wool
100% merino wool
Approximately 30m (33yds) per
    100g (3½oz) ball

Big Wool
Super chunky pure wool
100% merino wool
Approximately 80m (87yds) per
    100g (3½oz) ball

Big Wool Fusion
Super chunky pure wool
100% wool
Approximately 80m (87yds) per
    100g (3½oz) ball

Calmer
Soft cotton mix
75% cotton/25% acrylic/microfibre
Approximately 160m (175yds) per
    50g (1¾oz) ball

Cotton Braid
Chunky cotton mix
68% cotton/22% viscose/10%
    linen
Approximately 50m (55yds) per
    50g (1¾oz) ball

Cotton Glacé
Lightweight cotton yarn
100% cotton
Approximately 115m (125yds) per
    50g (1¾oz) ball

Cotton Rope
Chunky cotton mix
55% cotton/45% acrylic
Approximately 58m (63yds) per
    50g (1¾oz) ball

Felted Tweed
Lightweight double knitting
50% merino wool/25% alpaca/25%
    viscose
Approximately 175m (191yds) per
    50g (1¾oz) ball

Glimmer Print
Chunky cotton mix
50% cotton/22% viscose/10%
    linen
Approximately 40m (44yds) per
    50g (1¾oz) ball

Handknit DK Cotton
Medium-weight cotton yarn
100% cotton
Approximately 85m (92yds) per
    50g (1¾oz) ball

Holiday
Chunky cotton mix
56% cotton/37% viscose/7%
    polyester
Approximately 42m (46yds) per
    50g (1¾oz) ball

Kid Classic
Aran weight mohair mix
70% lambswool/26% kid mohair/
    4% nylon
Approximately 140m (153yds) per
    50g (1¾oz) ball

Kid Silk Haze
Very lightweight mohair yarn
70% super kid mohair/30% silk
Approximately 210m (230yds) per
    25g (1oz) ball

Kid Silk Night
Very lightweight mohair yarn
67% super kid mohair/18%
  silk/10% polyester/5% nylon
Approximately 208m (227yds) per
  25g (1oz) ball

Lurex Shimmer
Very lightweight lurex yarn
80% viscose/20% polyester
Approximately 95m (104yds) per
  25g (1oz) ball

Rowan Spray
Super chunky wool mix
60% wool/40% acrylic
Approximately 80m (87yds) per
  100g (3½oz) ball

Scottish Tweed DK
Pure Wool double knitting
100% pure new wool
Approximately 113m (123yds) per
  50g (1¾oz) ball

Scottish Tweed 4ply
Pure Wool 4ply
100% pure new wool
Approximately 110m (120yds) per
  25g (1oz) ball

Summer Tweed
Aran-weight silk and cotton yarn
70% silk/30% cotton
Approximately 108m (118yds) per
  50g (1¾oz) hank

Wool Cotton
Double-knitting-weight wool and
  cotton
50% merino wool/50% cotton
Approximately 113m (123yds) per
  50g (1¾oz) ball

4-ply cotton
Pure cotton 4ply
100% pure cotton
Approximately 170m (186yds) per
  50g (1¾oz) ball

4-ply Soft
Fine pure wool
100% merino wool
Approximately 175m (191yds) per
  50g (1¾oz) ball

CONVERSIONS

Needle sizes

US SIZE	METRIC SIZE	OLD UK & CANADIAN SIZE
15	10	000
13	9	00
11	8	0
11	7.5	1
10½	7	2
10½	6.5	3
10	6	4
9	5.5	5
8	5	6
7	4.5	7
6	4	8
5	3.75	9
4	3.5	–
3	3.25	10
2/3	3	11
2	2.75	12
1	2.25	13
0	2	14

Weights and lengths

oz = g × 0.0352
g = oz × 28.35
in = cm × 0.3937
cm = in × 2.54
yd = m × 0.9144
m = yd × 1.0936

ABBREVIATIONS

beg	beginning/begin
cont	continue
cm	centimetre
c4b	cable 4 back: slip next 2 sts onto a cable needle and hold at back of work, k2, then k2 from the cable needle
c4f	cable 4 front: slip next 2 sts onto a cable needle and hold at front of work, k2, then k2 from the cable needle
c6b	cable 6 back: slip next 3 sts onto a cable needle and hold at back of work, k3, then k3 from the cable needle
dec	decrease
g	grams
in	inch
inc	increase
k	knit
k2tog	knit two stitches together
k2togtbl	knit two stitches together through the back loop
mb	make bobble: using yarn B, (k1, p1) twice into next st, (turn, p4, turn, k4) twice, turn, p4, turn and sl2, k2tog, psso
mm	millimetre
m1	make one stitch
oz	ounces
p	purl
patt	pattern
pb	place bead: yarn forward, slip bead to front of work, slip 1 st purlwise, take yarn to back of work. Bead will now be sitting in front of slipped stitch
ps	Place sequin: yarn forward, slip sequin to front of work, slip 1 st purlwise, take yarn to back of work. Sequin will now be sitting in front of the slipped stitch
psso	pass slipped stitch over
p2sso	pass two slipped stitches over
p2tog	purl two stitches together
p2togtbl	purl two stitches together through back loop
rep	repeat
RS	right side of work
sl	slip
st st	stocking (stockinette) stitch
st/sts	stitch/stitches
WS	wrong side of work
yb	yarn back
yf	yarn forward
*	repeat instructions between * as many times as instructed
( )	repeat instructions between ( ) as many times as instructed.

Acknowledgements

Thank you to the following people for their help and support while working on this book:

Michelle Lo, Katie Cowan, and Katie Hudson at Collins & Brown, the entire team at Rowan for their constant support and wonderful yarns and to all my knitters with a special thank you to Rita who always manages to save the day with a bit of 'emergency knitting'! And last, but not least, I extend my gratitude to Jez without whose fantastic pompom making skills, let's face it, the book would be incomplete!

Thank you!

SUPPLIERS

Suppliers of Rowan Yarns and Jaeger Handknits

UK
Rowan Yarns and Jaeger Handknits
Green Lane Mill
Holmfirth
West Yorkshire
HD9 2DX
Tel: 01484 681881
www.knitrowan.com

USA
Westminster Fibers, Inc.
4 Townsend West,
Suite 8
Nashua, NH 03063
Tel: 603 886 5041
Fax: 603 886 1056
www.knitrowan.com
E-mail:
knitting@westminsterfibers.com

Canada
Diamond Yarn
9697 St Laurent
Montreal
Quebec H3L 2N1
Tel: 514 388 6188

Diamond Yarn (Toronto)
155 Martin Ross
Unit 3
Toronto
Ontario M3J 2L9
Tel: 416 736 6111

Australia
Rowan at Sunspun
185 Canterbury Road
Canterbury
Victoria 3126
Tel: 03 9830 1609

Suppliers of beads

UK
Beadworks (mail order)
16 Redbridge Enterprise Centre
Thompson Close
Ilford
Essex
IG1 1TY
Tel: 020 8553 3240
www.beadworks.co.uk

The Bead Shop
21a Tower Street
Covent Garden
London
WC2H 9NS
Tel: 020 7240 0931

The Brighton Bead Shop
(mail order)
21 Sydney Street
Brighton
BN1 4EN
Tel: 01273 675077
Email:
mailbox@beadsunlimited.co.uk
www.beadsunlimited.co.uk

Mill Hill Beads
www.millhillbeads.com

Creative Beadcraft Limited
(mail order)
Denmark Works
Sheepcote Dell Road
Beamond End
Near Amersham
Buckinghamshire
HP7 0RX
Tel: 01494 778818

Ells and Farrier
20 Beak Street
London
W1R 3HA
Tel: 0207 629 9964

USA
Global Beads
345 Castro Street
Mountain View, CA 94041
Tel: 650 967 7556
www.globalbeads.com

Keep Me In Stitches
77 Smithtown Boulevard
Smithtown, NY 11787
Tel: 631 724 8111
www.keepmeinstitches1.com